Prof CM
AR
B7
etal

Continuing Professional Education in
Librarianship and Other Fields:
A Classified and Annotated
Bibliography, 1965-1974

Garland Reference Library of the Humanities (Vol. 16)

Continuing Professional Education in Librarianship and Other Fields: A Classified and Annotated Bibliography, 1965-1974

Mary Ellen Michael

Garland Publishing, Inc., New York & London

1975

Library of Congress Cataloging in Publication Data

Michael, Mary Ellen.
    Continuing professional education in librarianship
and other fields.

    First published in a shorter version in Illinois
libraries, June, 1974, under title: A selected bibliography on continuing education 1965 to date.
    Includes index.
    1. Library education (Continuing education)--Bibli-
ography. 2. Professional education--Bibliography.
I. Title.
Z668.5.M53 1975   016.02'07   75-8998
ISBN 0-8240-1085-X

To Gary

TABLE OF CONTENTS*

*Numbers in parentheses refer to the number of articles
 in each section.

FOREWORD

The Illinois Library Association originally requested the Library Research Center at the University of Illinois, Urbana-Champaign, to compile a bibliography as part of a special issue of Illinois Libraries devoted to the subject of continuing education. It appeared in the June, 1974 issue as "A Selected Bibliography on Continuing Education 1965 to Date."

The following bibliography represents a more comprehensive literature survey in the area of continuing professional education for librarianship, with selected examples of continuing education in other professions.

I wish to thank Cathleen Palmini, who worked with me on the original bibliography; Olga Wise, who translated the German citations for this book; and Kathi Woomer and La Verne Caroline, who turned my handwritten cards into a finished manuscript. Last, but not least, my appreciation to Dr. Lucille M. Wert, Director of the Library Research Center, who encouraged me to proceed with this project.

PREFACE

The purpose of this preface is to assist the user of this bibliography in determining the extent to which it will meet his needs.

Scope and Coverage

The citations included herein represent a substantial portion of the theory and philosophy of continuing library science education published from 1965 to 1974. No attempt was made to cover all accounts of in-service training programs. The annotations describe the content of the work and do not evaluate the quality although it was sometimes tempting to do so. In-service training entries detail specific "how we did it" programs. In general, the bibliography is restricted to the 1965-1974 period. However, a few works published in 1965, 1966 deal with studies covering earlier years. Also, one item, although published in 1975, concerns a seminar on continuing education held in 1974. These works have been included because they were found to be especially pertinent to the subject matter of this bibliography.

Classification Scheme

Parts I and II cover continuing education in librarianship. Part I documents monographs, articles, reports of organizations, and others written in the United States; Part II features items relating to other countries.

Parts I and II are subdivided into two sections each.
Section A concerns theory and philosophy; Section B--
selected examples of in-service training programs. The
writings in Part III are representative examples of
philosophy and theory of continuing professional education
in other fields. All annotated citations are held by the
University of Illinois Library, Urbana-Champaign. ERIC
numbers are given for those items available on microfiche.

One limitation of the bibliography relates to the broad
classification of the items. No attempt was made to separate
research, bibliographies, theoretical formulations, and
practice. A citation might contain two or more of these
facets so that it would have been difficult to assign the
work to the most appropriate category.

Observations

Although this bibliography was not compiled for the
purpose of analyzing the literature of continuing professional education certain observations assert themselves.
Many citations in this bibliography document the need for
continuing education, its value, and importance. However,
there is little theoretical work concerning how adults learn,
are motivated or the nature of their subject area needs.
Few examples can be found of research into the structure of
continuing education. Many more articles purport to expli-
cate how to utilize the various theories and techniques about
which so little is known. Examples of in-service training
demonstrate the value of a certain program and the satisfaction of the participants. Unfortunately, many of the

in-service training programs do not build upon each other but
work on isolated experiences. Often no follow-up report
details the degree of successful transfer of learning to the
work environment. Hopefully, the national network proposed
by the National Commission on Libraries and Information
Science (entry no. 204) will solve some of these problems.

PART I

Continuing Professional Education in
Librarianship in the U.S.

A. Theory and Philosophy

1. Adams, S. "Operation Bootstrap: Medical Librarians and

Continuing Education." Kentucky Library Association

Bulletin. 32 (April 1968), 4-11.

The abundance of programs for continuing education in librarianship reflects the splintering of the profession into myriad special interest groups. The lack of coherence, planning, and progression represents the profession's failure to identify educational objectives of concern to the profession as a whole. Medical librarians share common goals with the medical, dental, and health professions for continuing education. The author, Deputy Director of the National Library of Medicine, cites the work of the Medical Library Association in continuing education.

2. Allen, Lawrence A. Continuing Education Needs of Special

Librarians. New York: Special Libraries Association.

(in press)

3. Allen, Lawrence A. "Education of the State Library

Consultant." Southeastern Librarian. 18 (Spring 1968),

42-48.

Few programs have been developed to improve the skills and competence of state library consultants. The author first details the changing role of these consultants who are shifting from a role of "doing" to that of "consulting". Recognizing the growing need for continuing education of the state library consultant, Dr. Allen describes a curriculum for an education program. Emphasis is placed upon the objectives, methods, and content of such education. The content includes study of the behavioral sciences, management and administration theory, and library specialization. This curriculum can be implemented through formal and informal education opportunities with the cooperation of library schools and state agencies.

4. Allen, Lawrence A. Evaluation of the Community Librarians'

    Training Courses. Albany, New York State Library,

    1966. 198 p. ED 024 406.

        This study is designed to: (1) evaluate the Community
    Librarians' Training Courses which were conducted for five
    years in New York State to train persons without profes-
    sional library training who were serving as librarians and
    (2) appraise the entire training program of the Library
    Extension Division in order to make recommendations and
    provide guidelines for future growth and development. A
    major conclusion of the evaluation is that the Library
    Extension Division has entered the training field with the
    initiation of the series for the community librarians but
    that it must extend this service to others in the field,
    including professional librarians.

5. Allen, Lawrence A. and Conroy, Barbara. "Social Inter-

    action Skills." Library Trends. 20 (July 1971), 78-91.

        In presenting this training subsystem, the authors
    draw upon their experience in conducting institutes and
    seminars throughout the United States. Since the library
    is essentially a human organization, social interaction
    skills are a necessary component. Organizational and
    personal goals are achieved when the staff are working
    cooperatively together. Skills can be taught to staff to
    enable them to interrelate effectively with clients and
    colleagues. The authors discuss the findings of applied
    behavioral science and propose a model of team building.

6. Alvarez, Robert S. "Continuing Education for the Public

    Librarian." California Librarian. 30 (July 1969),

    177-86.

        The author, Director of the San Francisco Public Li-
    brary, observes that while the main business of the li-
    brarian is to get other people to read, attend lectures,

take courses and keep abreast of new developments, the librarian himself is often less energetic in seeing to his
own continuing education. Librarians are often too slow
in accepting and implementing new ideas. Large city libraries do not reflect the changing needs of the population they serve in terms of the physical aspects of the
building, hours open, attitudes of staff, etc. The author
does not believe that acquiring the Ph.D. is the answer
but rather a type of instruction that stimulates and in-
spires people to ask questions, to become tolerant of
other people's ideas and to be critical and questioning
of their own present methods. Commercial businesses are
already actively engaged in continuing education for their
employees. Librarians working through library schools and
library association should be similarly organized.

7. Alvarez, Robert S.; Boaz, Martha; Duncan, Margaret; Kenney,

   Louis A. "Continuing Education for Librarians."

   California Librarian. 30 (July 1969), 177-202.

   The four articles stress the urgency of providing continuing education for the public, special, and academic
librarian. Continuing education should get people to
relate the things they hear and see at meetings to their
own library situation, and make them feel that they can
and should do something about these ideas. For the
special librarian, it is recommended that he become
conscious of the desirability of training in the principles
of administration. Each librarian should consider each
library function as a part of a whole. Systems analysis
would provide the kind of analytical thinking needed to
overcome a compartmentalized view of library work.

8. American Association of School Librarians. School Library

   Personnel Task Analysis. Illinois: American Library

   Association, 1969.

9. American Association of School Librarians. Supervisors

    Section. "Questionnaire about Continuing Education

    for School Library Media Supervisors." School

    Libraries. 18 (Summer 1969), 53.

    The American Association of School Librarians (AASL)
inserted a questionnaire in School Libraries soliciting
the opinions of school library media supervisors concerning
continuing education. The AASL published a summary sheet
of responses based upon the findings of this questionnaire.

10. American Library Association. Activities Committee on New

    Directions for ALA. Final Report of the Activities

    Committee on New Directions for ALA. Chicago:

    American Library Association, 1970. 94p.

    This committee of the ALA makes major recommendations
concerning the organization's philosophy, priorities for
action, organizational structure, and changing interests
of its membership. In the area of continuing education,
the committee lists six means for the encouragement of professional growth of its members. The ALA could: 1) sponsor
a wide range of workshops and seminars; 2) prepare packaged
multi-media programs for professional updating; 3) design
and produce programmed instructional courses for sale to
members; 4) make known opportunities outside ALA for
continuing education experiences; 5) lend advisory and
consultative services to local libraries and library
agencies wanting to develop continuing education programs;
and 6) coordinate all ALA activities concerned with professional upgrading of librarians.

11. American Library Association. Association of State Library

Agencies and Library Education Division. Interdivision

Committee on Education of State Library Personnel.

Education of State Library Personnel; A Report with

Recommendations Relating to the Continuing Education

of State Library Agency Professional Personnel.

American Library Association, 1971. 62p.

This committee report examines the continuing education
needs of state library professional personnel. Most of
the report can be applied equally well to all levels of
library personnel in all types of libraries. The greatest
immediate need is for the continuing education of consultants. The committee recommends an initial program
for state library consultants which would provide the
basis for a continuing education program for all state
library professional personnel.

12. American Library Association. Committee on Accreditation.

Standards for Accreditation, 1972. Adopted by the

Council of the American Library Association

June 27, 1972; effective January 1, 1973. Chicago:

American Library Association, 1972.

13. American Library Association. "Guidelines to the Develop-

ment of Human Resources in Libraries: Rationale,

Policies, Programs and Recommendations." Library

Trends. 20 (July 1971), 97-117.

The Guidelines postulate that an individual library system can strengthen its role in the development of human resources by developing from a systems point of view, a philosophy, policies, and programs in the area of human resources development; and, making sure they are known and practiced throughout the system. Personnel development and continuing education are shared responsibilities in the profession. The committee makes some recommendations to implement such planning for other groups--state and federal agencies, library schools, and professional associations.

14. American Library Association. Library Administration Division. Personnel Administration Section. Staff Development Committee. Guidelines Subcommittee. "Developing a Model for Continuing Education and Personnel Development in Libraries." Library Trends. 20 (July 1971), 92-96.

A model is presented for use by librarians in analyzing basic needs and problems, and in developing the framework for a program of personnel development and continuing education which will make possible the use of managerial techniques. The model is adaptable to any size or type of library or library system, or group of cooperating libraries.

15. American Library Association. Library Education and Manpower; A Statement of Policy Adopted by the Council of the American Library Association. June 30, 1970. Chicago: Office of Library Education, American Library Association, 1970. p.(8) Paragraphs 33-35.

16. American Library Association, Library Education Division.

    Interdivision Committee on Training Programs for

    Supportive Library Staff. "Criteria for Programs to

    Prepare Library Technical Assistants." Wisconsin

    Library Bulletin. 65 (September-October 1969), 359-66.

    This report, approved by the Board of Directors of
the American Library Association, is its official policy
regarding criteria for programs to train library technical
assistants. The Library Education Division (LED) developed
these guidelines for individuals responsible for planning
programs for library technical assistants, and for the
evaluation of existing programs for library technical
assistants. "The programs are conceived as introductory
preparation of personnel to fill beginning positions in
the range of technical assistant positions in a variety of
situations.

17. Annual Report of the Southwestern Library Interestate

    Cooperative Endeavor [SLICE] Project of the South-

    western Library Association 91st, October 1, 1971 to

    December 31, 1972); and Final Report for Council on

    Library Resources, 1972. 152 p. ED 072 783.

    One of the topics discussed in this annual report is
the continuing education program for librarians. The
focus of the program is on improving library services to
the disadvantaged ethnic groups and a systematic planning
and evaluation methodology.

18. Asheim, Lester E. "Education and Manpower for Librarian-

ship; First Steps Toward a Statement of Policy."

ALA Bulletin. 62 (October 1968), 1096-1106.

The Library profession must establish and maintain
standards and norms for the preparation of people who work
at every level in libraries. This includes not only the
"professional" but also clerical and preprofessional staff.

Asheim advocates two professional levels, supported
by subprofessional, technical and clerical staff.
The two classes of professionals would be: 1) librarian
(with a master's degree) and 2) professional specialist
(e.g., subject or language specialist, information
scientist, administrator) with training beyond the master's,
such as a sixth year post master's education at a library
school, a doctorate, a master's in another subject, or
continuing education for librarianship in the form of
institutes and short courses. Clerical, technical and
subprofessional norms are also discussed.

19. Asheim, Lester. "Library Activities in the Field of

Manpower, 1967." In: Lester Asheim, ed. Library

Manpower Needs and Utilization. Chicago: American

Library Association, 1967. 16-19.

A questionnaire was sent to the fifty state library
agencies to ascertain what programs, if any, they had
specifically directed to the shortage of manpower in the
library field (1967). Three states reported no program
for the encouragement of continuing education. Others
reported a range of activities from attendance at professional meetings to an extensive research project in Maryland.
In-service programs, scholarships, and grants-in-aid programs are cited. The conclusion is made that too little
is being done in continuing education.

20. Association of American Library Schools. Annual Meeting

    of the Association of American Library Schools for

    the Continuing Library Education Network. AALS,

    Committee on Continuing Library Education, January 28,

    1973.

    A mini (four-hour) workshop was held in order to learn
    what is being done in other professions and disciplines
    regarding continuing professional education with the hope
    that some concepts and ideas might be applicable to the
    library profession.

21. Association of American Library Schools. Committee on

    Continuing Library Education. "Proposed Working

    Statement on Continuing Education for the Profession."

    Approved by the AALS Executive Board, October, 1973.

22. Association of American Library Schools. Continuing

    Library Education Study Committee. Summary Report,

    January 1972, Annual Meeting. Journal of Education

    for Librarianship, 12 (Spring 1972), 267-69.

    Comment by R. N. Case. Journal of Education for

    Librarianship, 12 (Spring 1972), 269-72.

    The summary report presents assumptions on the value
    of continuing education for librarians, objectives for
    implementation, and recommendations for implementation.

23. Association of American Library Schools. "Position Paper

   on Continuing Library Education." Special Libraries.

   64 (December 1973), 580-81.

   This outline summarizes the committee work of the AALS
on the subject of continuing education to date. The basic
assumptions made by the committee are broad--the need for
continuing education; general statements concerning its
objectives and content; and the organizational structure
for continuing education. Coordination and cooperation
will be necessary among five components--individual
librarians, state, regional and national library and information associations, library schools, the libraries, and
state, regional and national agencies.

24. Association of American Library Schools. "Standing Com-

   mittee on Continuing Library Education." Journal of

   Education for Librarianship. 13 (Fall 1972), 137-44.

   Summarized are the minutes of the Standing Committee
on Continuing Library Education of the American Association of Library Schools. A position paper was adopted
and a network of liaison people from library associations
and library schools was established. The liaison representatives and the library school they represent are
listed herein.

25. Association of American Library Schools. Study Committee

   on the Role of the AALS in Continuing Library Educa-

   tion. Tentative Draft of a Position Paper. 1972.

   38 p.

   The AALS makes recommendations for the implementation
of a program for continuing library education both inside
AALS and in cooperation with other relevant groups. The

appendix lists the goals, criteria, and components of
national planning for continuing education of librarians
and provides a discussion of "What is continuing education?"

26. Association of Research Libraries. Office of University

Library Management Studies. "Management Review and

Analysis Program." Washington, D.C.: Association

of Research Libraries, 1972.

27. Association of Research Libraries. Office of University

Library Management Studies. "Review of Planning

Activities in Academic and Research Libraries."

ARL Management Supplement, Number One. Washington,

D.C.: Association of Research Libraries, 1972.

28. Association of Research Libraries. Office of University

Library Management Studies. A Summary of the Results

of the Office of Management Studies Survey of the

Recruitment, Staff Development, and Minority Employ-

ment Practices of ARL Libraries, 1972.

29. Barzun, Jacques. "The New Librarian to the Rescue."

Library Journal. 94 (November 1, 1969), 3963-65.

Professor Barzun proposes the restoration of the role
of librarian as generalist. The librarian must become the
librarian reader-and-teacher, leaving the role of technician to the computer. The librarian should not be a

subject specialist but a generalist. He should not merely
provide technical information about the physical location
of books. He must have a firsthand knowledge of their
contents and their value. The New Librarian must be the
selector of books and pruner of collections, and for this
his associations with scholars and students must be
genuine and continuous. The author recommends that the
great public libraries cooperate with colleges and uni-
versites in the training of such librarians in reading
programs. Barzun rejects the Ph.D. as too narrow an
expertise and opts for the well-read individual who can
impart the exact and expert communication of intelligence.

30. Belzer, Jack. "Information Science Education: Curriculum

    Development and Evaluation." American Documentation.

    20 (October 1969), 325-76.

    The Curriculum Committee of the Special Interest Group
on Education in Information Science of the American Society
for Information Science met at the University of Pittsburgh
in an effort to develop standards for curricula in information science. The objectives of the conference were
to define the professional pursuits of each area of
specialization in information science and to identify
the knowledge required for professional practice in each.
Two groups were formed. One group was information science
oriented in the pure sense, the other information systems
oriented. The papers of the speakers are presented here.

31. Bennett, H. H. "Continuing Education: A Survey of Staff

    Development Programs." School Libraries. 19

    (Spring 1970), 11-20.

    The states have accepted responsibility for initiating
in-service programs for school librarians. The one-day
or the one-week regional workshop has been the mode for
developing school library staff. Federal programs, the
library school, professional associations, and the local

education agency have also sponsored in-service training.
At the local level, self-evaluation can be used as a
pattern for improvement. Procedure manuals, checklists
or surveys, and the newsletter can be instruments of
self-evaluation. Closed circuit television used as a
teaching tool and activities which center on developing
standards are also methods of continuing professional
growth. Three essentials for a successful staff development program are financial support, released time, and
commendation or a tangible benefit.

32. Boaz, Martha T. "Continuing Education." Drexel Library

     Quarterly. 3 (April 1967), 151-57.

     The author describes the varying forms of continuing
education, the types of programs offered by agencies--
extension courses in library schools, NDEA institutes,
etc. Research is needed in the following areas of continuing education for librarians: 1) the organizational
structure including the types of programs offered, subjects covered, admission requirements, faculty competencies,
costs and financing, time duration, levels at which offered,
and credit given; 2) the purposes of the programs and the
methods used to achieve objectives; 3) the tangible and
intangible values derived for the individual and his institution; and 4) the effect of continuing education on
society.

33. Boaz, Martha T. "Education A-Go-Go Continuing . . ."

     California Librarian. 30 (July 1969), 187-90.

     "The education of today is obsolete before it is
current!" Knowledge is accelerating. No one is well
educated unless he continues to seek learning. The author
describes some predicted trends in education, science and
technology.

     Librarians need to become more confident that library
technicians can do work formerly done by librarians. Librarians would then have more time for planning and research.

34. Bobinski, George S. "Report of Continuing Education Com-

        mittee of the School of Information and Library

        Studies." Buffalo, New York: State University of

        New York at Buffalo, 1972. (Mimeographed)

35. Boelke, Joanne. <u>Library Technicians: A Survey of Current

        Developments. Review Series no. 1</u>. Minneapolis:

        University of Minnesota, 1968. 12p. ED 019 530.

     This survey summarizes current programs for library
technicians in this emerging field; presents an overview
of the issues and problems of the subject; enumerates the
organizations and agencies concerned with library technicians, and lists a selective bibliography that reflects
current trends. Data are based on correspondence with
people active in the field as well as an examination of
the literature. Both sources indicate that all types of
libraries are employing technicians in increasing numbers;
the role of the technician is controversial; organizations
for library technicians are being formed; professional
associations, the U.S. Office of Education, and others
are sponsoring studies, surveys, and conferences; and
there is a rise in the number of training programs.

36. Bone, Larry E. and Hartz, Frederic R. "Taking the Full

        Ride: A Librarian's Routes to Continuing Education."

        <u>Library Journal</u>. 95 (October 1970), 3244-46.

     New and experienced librarians must meet four require-
ments to keep abreast of the field: 1) be able to guide
and interpret needs and programs; 2) know as much about
the new media as is known about books; 3) understand the
political, social, financial, and informational requirements of the community, and 4) understand and apply sound
principles of management.

To meet these requirements librarians have several
alternative avenues of learning through continuing education programs--a separate master's degree in a cognate
field, a sixth year certificate program in a library school,
a doctorate, institutes, workshops, and short conferences.

37. Booz, Allen and Hamilton, Inc. Organization and Staffing

of the Libraries of Columbia University: A Case

Study. Sponsored by the Association of Research Li-

braries in Cooperation with the American Council on

Education, under a grant from the Council on Library

Resources. Westport, Connecticut: Redgrave Informa-

tion Resources Corp., 1973. 210 p.

The purposes of this case study are to: 1) project
the future needs of the Columbia University Libraries;
2) evaluate their existing organization and staffing;
3) recommend desirable principles of executive staffing
and organization; 4) suggest a plan of library organization;
and 5) lay out a detailed staffing pattern for the Columbia
University Libraries. This well documented report describes
current trends in higher education and their implications
for libraries. Some of the recommendations in the report
are the provision of new staff specialties in order to
add new capabilities to library programs; the formation of
new career patterns allowing for individual pursuit of
scholarly, professional, or administrative interests; and
orientation and in-service training for staff at all
levels on a continuing basis.

38. Breivik, Patricia Senn, ed. "Continuing Education."

Journal of Education for Librarianship. 14 (Winter

1974), 201-02.

The editors of the above journal have initiated a
column on continuing education. This issue is its first

appearance. The American Association of Library Schools
has established a Committee on Continuing Library Education which is complemented in its efforts by its Continuing
Library Education Network of representatives from the
library schools and library associations. The purpose of
this column will be to serve as a forum on the broad topic
of continuing education for librarianship. It will serve
as a clearinghouse for information regarding innovative
programs whether sponsored by associations, libraries, or
library schools.

39. Breivik, Patricia Senn, ed. "Continuing Education."

    Journal of Education for Librarianship. 15 (Summer

    1974), 67-69.

    At the annual ALA conference in New York, the Program
Planning Committee of the Information Science and Automation Division (ISAD) of ALA met with representatives of
library schools to discuss ways in which they could both
cooperate in providing continuing education opportunities
for its membership.

    ISAD can benefit its own membership by cooperating
with library schools. ISAD hopes to eliminate one or both
of the major expenses involved--rental of space for the
program and housing for participants. It is also seeking
"the talent of selected graduate schools" as resources for
faculty and program planning. Financial considerations
have not been resolved, so the possibility of offering
a series of tutorial seminars was not finalized. The
consensus at the end of the meeting was that the committee would consider brief outlines of short-term institutes which would fall under ISAD's general area of
interest. Only programs which could be replicated at
other locations would be considered.

40. Brodman, Estelle. "A Philosophy of Continuing Education."

    Bulletin of the Medical Library Association. 56

    (April 1968), 145-49.

Continuing education affects the individual, the library in which he works, and the user of the library.
Librarians are finding that their traditional functions,
accepted without question twenty years ago, are no longer
valid in a rapidly changing society. Professional associations need to set forth a philosophy which includes an
emphasis on continuing education.

41. Brodman, Estelle. "Why Continuing Education?" District

   of Columbia Libraries. 37 (Fall 1966), 51-54.

   The author gives a brief overview of the development
of continuing education from colonial times. She
stresses the need for librarians to develop their critical
faculties and keep abreast of the new machine methods in
cataloging and audiovisual services.

42. Bundy, Mary Lee and Wasserman, Paul. "Professionalism

   Reconsidered." College and Research Libraries.

   29 (January 1968), 5-26.

   There are three important relationships of a profes-
sional--client, organizational, and professional ones.
Accepted criteria and norms determine what constitutes
professional practice. The application of these standards
to librarianship finds the profession wanting. Librarians
perform some subprofessional work routines in their work
and are treated as inferiors in their bureaucratic relationships. Library schools and professional associations
also play a part in the process of professionalization;
their role is discussed herein. The future of librarianship as a profession depends on the evaluation of these
problems.

43. Burnham, Reba M. <u>The Role of the Supervisor in Professiona</u>

<u>Growth and Development</u>. Paper presented at the

American Library Association Annual Meeting. (New Yor

1974). Clearwater, Florida: Pinellas County Board

of Public Instruction, 1974. 18p. ED 094 795.

   Educational leaders need to keep up-to-date in their
field and progress in their supervisory methods. A team
approach is needed for supervision in schools. A professional supervisor encourages each member of the school
staff to perform leadership tasks and respects their status
as professionals. Supervisors need to keep themselves informed about trends toward competency-based education of
all school personnel and methods of applying this information to their own staff.

44. Case, Robert N., and Lowrey, Anna Mary. <u>School Library</u>

<u>Manpower Project: A Report on Phase I</u>. Chicago:

American Library Association, 1971.

45. Center for Documentation and Communication Research. <u>Educa-</u>

<u>tion for Hospital Library Personnel: Feasibility Stud</u>

<u>for Continuing Education of Medical Librarians</u>.

(Interim Report No. 2 and Interim Report No. 3).

Cleveland, Ohio: Case Western Reserve University,

1968.

46. Christianson, Elin. Paraprofessional and Nonprofessional

    Staff in Special Libraries. SLA State-of-the-Art

    Review no. 2. New York: Special Libraries Associa-

    tion, 1973. 70p.

    This study reviews research on nonprofessional per-
sonnel in special librarianship and pertinent research on
paraprofessionals (library technical assistants) in other
fields in order to determine the present situation in
this phase of special librarianship, and to identify areas
that need further study. One study reported here is manpower utilization in health sciences libraries. Staffing
patterns were determined by type of library, educational
and experiential backgrounds, and involvement of professional and nonprofessional personnel. Although most nonprofessionals have no prior work or subject experience upon
taking a position in a special library, librarians feel
that nonprofessionals have much to contribute if they receive special training.

47. Clark, Philip M. and Johnson, Mildred Y. A Training Pro-

    gram for Library Associates in Maryland.

    New Brunswick, N.J.: Bureau of Library and Informa-

    tion Science Research, Graduate School of Library

    Service, Rutgers University, 1971.

48. Cohn, William L. "Library Education in the Seventies."

    Wisconsin Library Bulletin. 69 (July 1973), 222-23.

    Library education will become a matter of continuing
education. One year of formal study is not adequate to
meet the increasing complexity of library science. Continuing education will take several forms in the seventies--
sixth year degrees and doctoral studies; institutes and

seminars with a short completion time; association meetings; courses in subject areas or computer science taken
by the individual on his own initiative. In the seventies,
the subject of automation will be a strong focus for
continuing education to acquaint librarians with the
potential of its use. Continuing education is critically
needed in management where libraries are held accountable
for budgets and quality of service.

49. "Conference on In-training of Library and Information Staff

1970, Imperial College." [papers] Aslib Proceedings.

22 (June 1970), 256-87.

These papers presented at a one-day conference cover
the following topics: the practical problems and principles
of in-service training; in-service training in the ASLIB
Library and Information Department; cooperative schemes
for in-service training; and others.

50. Conroy, Barbara and others. Leadership for Change; A Report

of the Outreach Leadership Network. Durham,

New Hampshire, New England Center for Continuing

Education, 1972. 187p. ED 071 671.

The Outreach Leadership Network (OLN) was a regional
program of continuing education for public librarians in
New England. Federally funded under the Higher Education
Act, the project began July 1971 through October 1972.
Its goal was to provide for more effective programs of
public library services directed toward presently un-
served community groups. OLN sought to provide educational
programs to actively extend library services to more
citizens than presently were being served. This outreach program also served as a training ground for the
development of public library leaders--librarians not only
committed to outreach service but also skilled in program
planning and in working with groups.

51. Conroy, Barbara. Staff Development and Continuing Educa-

tion Programs for Library Personnel: Guidelines

and Criteria. ERIC Clearinghouse on Library and

Information Sciences, Washington, D.C. National

Institute of Education, Division of HEW. 1973.

26p. ED 083 986.

All types of libraries face the common dilemma of
delineating and administering manpower resources
effectively. Manpower is becoming the most essential resource as librarianship moves toward increased service
orientation. Continuing education and staff development
are a partial solution but evidence of current efforts
is not promising. The goal of the guidelines is to
formulate an overview of the basic tenets for a systematic
plan of continuing education and staff development of library personnel. The guidelines and criteria are practical
rather than theoretical and can be used as a working tool
toward the development of the human potential within the
library profession. The guidelines are applicable to new
or existing programs for planning, implementing, and
evaluating manpower development programs.

52. Continuing Education--A Self-Evaluation Checklist.

Education for Librarianship Committee. New Jersey

Library Association. 1972 (Mimeographed)

The New Jersey Library Association's Education for
Librarianship Committee has prepared a checklist of eight
questions. It serves as a self-evaluation form for administrators in all types of libraries. The questions
cover library policies on continuing education for staff
(written, understood, or in contract form); time off and
tuition paid to attend courses, state, and national
conventions; types of in-service training provisions
made for feedback from staff who attend courses, conferences, and others.

53.   Continuing Education in Librarianship Newsletter.

University of Kentucky, Office for Continuing Educa-

tion of Library Science, December 17, 1973.

This is the first issue of an irregular publication
dependent upon the amount and relevancy of news about
continuing education in Kentucky and other states. It includes not only news items, but a calendar of continuing
education activities of interest to Kentucky librarians
and library related personnel.

54.   "Continuing Education in the Southwest." Library Journal.

(March 1, 1974), 611.

Allie Beth Martin, Director of the Tulsa City-County
Library, was the project coordinator for a survey of continuing education in the six Southwestern states. One
recommendation made is that the Southwestern Library
Association "assume responsibility for developing a
meaningful and viable continuing education program for
. . . the region." The program should be developed
"cooperatively with state, regional, and national groups,
library schools, employing institutions, and individuals."

Excerpts of the report can be obtained from Marion
Mitchell, SWLA Exec. Secy., Box 36206, Airlawn Station,
Dallas, Texas 75235. (May 1974).

55.   "Continuing Education Plan for Thirteen Western States."

Library Journal. 93 (April 15, 1968), 1570.

An interstate master plan for continuing professional
education of working librarians, its aim is to integrate
existing educational resources in the region as well as
suggest new ones. Advancement of the professional education of librarians regardless of assignment or type of
library will be the intention.

56. Cornell University Libraries. "Report on the Committee

on Continuing Education and Professional Growth."

Ithaca: Cornell University, 1969. 51p. ED 056 718.

Seven areas are of importance in this report: 1) bibliographical control; 2) need for changes in the library's organizational structure to meet new challenges; 3) professionalism; 4) reappraisal of supporting staff in terms of strengthening their roles; 5) management training available to all supervisory personnel; 6) the application of computers to library operations; and 7) programmed instruction and gaming simulation for use in library instruction.

57. Dalton, Jack. "Library Education and Research in

Librarianship: Some Current Problems and Trends in

the United States." Paper presented at the 35th

session of the IFLA General Council, Copenhagen,

Denmark, August 1969. Libri. 19 (No. 3, 1969), 157-67.

Four major points are discussed: 1) some of the significant developments that have occurred in professional education in library science during the sixties; 2) the impact of electronic data processing machinery on curricula and research programs of the library schools; 3) trends in the recruiting and training of library school teachers in the sixties and the predicted needs for the seventies; and 4) the place of the traditional curricula of existing library schools in planning for the future and the possibility of a new structure of institutions with levels of training to cope with the developing need of libraries and information centers.

58. Dalton, Jack. "Observations on Advance Study Programs in
    the Library Schools of the United States." In:

    Larry E. Bone, ed., Library Education: An Inter-

    national Survey. Champaign, Ill.: University of

    Illinois Graduate School of Library Science, 1968.

    pp. 317-28.

This article concentrates on the recurring problems
of U.S. graduate education and points to a dilemma in the
goals of advanced study in librarianship--is the purpose
of doctoral study academic or professional? Is it for
college teaching or for research? The evolution of the
doctoral program is given with special emphasis on library
schools. The varying philosophies of admission standards,
curricula, types of degrees awarded, recruiting, and
financial considerations are discussed.

59. Damtoft, Finn. "Continuing Education: Our Baby." APLA
    Bulletin. 33 (June 1969), 21-24.

Effective continuing education can be achieved. The
individual librarian and the library administration work
together with the latter as the driving force. The library administration must play a central role for two
reasons: 1) there will be no staff interest in continuing
education without the establishment of formal programs as
a natural part of the work assignment and unless rewards
for increased knowledge and competency are provided; and
2) only the administration has the financial and organizational resources to support such programs by granting money, guaranteeing time allowances, and providing
laboratory facilities. The administration can encourage
participation which will allow staff members to periodically
review their knowledge of the existing system, to have a
staff bulletin listing new programs, and, a monitoring
system which would evaluate the validity of a program
during the operating period.

60. Danton, J. Periam. <u>Between M.L.S. and Ph.D.; A Study of</u>

<u>Sixth-Year Specialist Programs in Accredited Library</u>

<u>Schools</u>. Chicago: American Library Association, 1970.

103p.

The purpose of this survey is to describe educational
practice in the emerging sixth-year specialist programs in
library schools accredited by the American Library Association. Chapter 1 provides a brief historical overview of
formal library education programs from 1927 to 1960 and the
relationship of these programs to the sixth-year degree
inaugurated in 1961. Chapter 2 describes the scope and
method of the study. Chapter 3 is a description of the
twenty schools that have sixth-year specialist programs.
Chapter 5 covers evaluation. The Appendices contain the
list of library schools surveyed, the questionnaires, and
other forms used in the study.

61. Davis, Richard A. "Continuing Education: Formal and In-

formal." <u>Special Libraries</u>. 58 (January 1967), 27-30.

Continuing education can be both formal and informal.
In either case it can be haphazard or directed. Whether
formal or informal, continuing education requires that the
librarian have a goal in mind and a plan for achieving it.
In arriving at the plan it is helpful to have an advisor.
With a goal and a plan the librarian has to think about
means. Those interested in continuing education for librarianship need to consider new and imaginative avenues,
rather than depend on traditional, not always satisfactory
techniques.

62. DeProspo, Ernest R., Jr. "Contributions of the Political

Scientist and Public Administrator to Library Adminis-

tration." In: <u>Administration and Change: Continuing</u>

<u>Education in Library Administration</u>. New Brunswick,

New Jersey: Rutgers University Press, 1969. pp. 29-38.

The library administrator lacks familiarity with the more recent findings and ideas in the field of administration because of lack of contact with other professions. The political scientist and the public administrator can be of great help. The authors suggest the following: 1) adapt the literature in the field which can be integrated into the library literature; 2) encourage continuing education for library administrators by bringing in those skills which library administrators have indicated they need to have in order to improve their ideas and skills; and 3) improve library services through better planning.

63. DeProspo, Ernest R., Jr. and Huang, Theodore S. "Continuing Education for the Library Administrator: His Needs." Administration and Change: Continuing Education in Library Administration. New Brunswick, New Jersey: Rutgers University Press, 1969. pp. 21-27.

The results of a questionnaire are summarized. Its purpose was to study possible programs of continuing education in administration for chief librarians. The three means most frequently checked by which librarians acquired new ideas and skills in administration are: 1) read books and articles; 2) attend workshops and institutes; and 3) consult experts. There is a substantial drop-off after these three selections. "Discussions with colleagues," "professional meetings," and "visits to other libraries" received fewer responses. This finding suggests that not many "new ideas" and "solutions" are passed out in these face-to-face relationships nor is there a continual exchange of repeated ideas. In addition, the finding indicates that workshops, institutes, readings, etc., have not provided librarians with different ways of looking at their administrative problems.

64. Dillon, Richard H. "Phantom of the Library: The Creative

     Subject Specialist." In: Louisiana State University,

     Baton Rouge. Libraries. Library Lectures: Numbers

     Nine through Sixteen, November 1967-April 1970.

     The Library. 1971. pp. 100-15.

   Librarianship suffers as a sub-profession because librarians are generalists and not creative subject specialists.
   Too many areas of knowledge and information are covered too
   thinly by too little subject competence. Librarianship
   needs to be more humanized, more innovative, and more
   creative. The author rejects the Ph.D. as a solution to
   the problem because it is too narrow and stultifying an
   experience. Instead, he prefers an individual with a
   double master's degree in librarianship and a subject
   field. The true subject specialist will not only be
   content oriented but will be both intellectually and
   emotionally involved in his work of service orientation
   to the users of the library. Working from a strong base
   of subject knowledge, he will be open to using all forms
   of media and hardware and not feel threatened by automation and computers. Library schools need to re-evaluate
   their curriculums and place more emphasis on specialist
   education.

65. Donahugh, Robert H., and others. Report of the Commission

     on Continuing Education, Kent State University,

     School of Library Science. Kent, Ohio: Kent State

     University, School of Library Science, 1971.

66. Downs, Robert B. "Education for Librarianship in the United

    States and Canada." In: Larry E. Bone, ed., Library

    Education: An International Survey. Champaign, Ill.:

    University of Illinois Graduate School of Library

    Science, 1968. pp. 1-20.

        This paper traces the evolution of professional li-
    brary education with the emergence of Melvil Dewey's
    School of Library Economy at Columbia University in 1887
    to the present proliferation of graduate library schools.
    The main focus concerns library education in the United
    States with only brief mention of Canada. Some topics
    discussed are the problems involved in determining
    accreditation policies, standards, the value of doctoral
    programs in library science, librarians considered as
    generalists or specialists, the critical shortage of
    trained librarians, and the growing emphasis on technology
    in library operations.

67. Drennan, Henry T. and Darling, Richard I. Library Manpower:

    Occupational Characteristics of Public and School Li-

    brarians. Washington, D.C.: United States Office

    of Education, 1966. 21p.

        This study of the occupational characteristics of
    public librarians is part of a larger survey, the Post-
    censal Study of Professional and Technical Manpower, which
    aims at identifying significant characteristics of many
    different kinds of professional and technical workers.
    The data in this report give a good deal of information
    about the amount and kinds of education the respondents
    received. This presentation attempts to delineate some
    of the emerging trends in the occupational characteristics
    of public and school librarians in the early 1960's.

68. Duncan, Margaret. "Making the Special Librarian Special:

The Case for Continuing Education." California

Librarian. 30 (July 1969), 191-98.

Library school fulfills the expertise needed in reference, cataloging, and the other techniques of library service; but continuing education is needed in the following areas: training in the principles of administration, systems analysis to consider each library function as a part of the whole, knowledge of the subjects which make his special library unique, and a thorough knowledge of the organization served by the library. The author then suggests ways in which these needs can be met through continuing education.

69. "Educational Technology Bill Pushes Planning and Training."

Library Journal. 98 (September 1, 1973), 2387.

Senator Thomas Eagleton (D-Mo.) has introduced a bill which stresses the need for planning and training rather than for more acquisition of materials. Eagleton observes that school and college classrooms do not make effective use of the rapid improvement in educational technology. The Educational Technology Act would put a two-year moratorium on purchases in favor of staff training. Four year plans would need to be submitted before schools and colleges would become eligible for staff training funds.

70. Fancher, Evelyn P. and Hudson, Earline H. "Continuing

Education Programs for Librarians in Tennessee: A

Survey." Tennessee Librarian. 24 (Summer 1972), 125-26.

Herein are the results of a survey questionnaire intended to determine the status of continuing education programs of academic, public, special, and school libraries in Tennessee. Topics covered include: types of programs, who participates, in what areas the strongest need for continuing education is felt, and funding of the programs.

71. Fast, Elizabeth T. "The Supervisor's Section." School

Libraries. 19 (Spring 1970), 47-48.

Reported here are the final results of a survey of
school library media supervisors analyzing their preferences in continuing education. Supervisors rate their
need for more information concerning management philosophy
and techniques as the most important, followed by curriculum
trends. Supervisors are most interested in short-term
workshops because of time constraints. Some school
districts will pay for workshop expenses directly or through
a jump in the salary scale after completion of the institute.

72. Fenland, Patrick R. Leadership Development for Librarians.

University of Pittsburgh, Pittsburgh, Pennsylvania,

1971. 112p. ED 054 840.

The purpose of this manual is to provide a guide to
the in-service training of librarians for community liaison
through the group work process. The manual was developed
for the supervisor participants in the Institute on
Discovery Management for Supervisors of Library Branches
Serving the Underprivileged and Emerging Communities.

73. Fleisher, Eugene. "Systems for Individual Study: Decks,

Cassettes, Dials or Buffers?" Library Journal.

96 (February 1971), 695-98.

Various kinds of individual study systems are
discussed. Recommendations for their use are made depend-
ing on the needs of the user and the learning situation
involved. Items discussed are individual checkout,
cassettes, loop transmissions, centralized systems,
central manual switching, dial-access retrieval, random
access retrieval, and combining systems.

74. Florida State University. Leadership Training Institute,

    School of Library Science. <u>Narrative Evaluation</u>

    <u>Report on the Leadership Training Institute</u>.

    Tallahassee: University of Florida, 1973.

    Funded under the HEA Title II-B the Leadership Train-
ing Institute (LTI) is under the direction of Dr. Harold
Goldstein. LTI has no scheduled academic training program, no enrolled participants, and no instructional staff.
LTI's purpose is to identify and meet library leadership
training needs as expressed by institute directors and
faculty as well as key library and media personnel. LTI's
plan includes the development of specialized leadership
training programs; preparation and distribution of leadership development materials, sharing of information between
institutes; reporting on seminars in management training;
and technical assistance to training institutes through
site visits.

    This one-year evaluation discusses several aspects
of the LTI program: its objectives, the participants,
staff, program activities, product development, facilities,
and consultants. The extensive appendices give site
visit reports, evaluation forms used, and sample agenda
for the training sessions.

75. Frasure, Kenneth J. <u>Your Leadership Development Program</u>.

    Paper presented at the Annual Conference at the

    American Association of School Administrators.

    Atlantic City, New Jersey. February, 1968, 22p.

    ED 021 330.

    The Federal government, state education divisions,
and universities have not placed enough emphasis on in-
service education for school administrators. Recent

studies in educational administration, especially in leadership development, could be applied in continuing education programs. Recommendations are offered for upgrading programs on leadership development.

76. Fristoe, Ashley J. "Doubling the Halflife" [letter].

Southeastern Librarian. 15 (Fall 1965), 124-25.

The author, an acquisitions librarian, comments on the problem of professional obsolescence due to the knowledge explosion. While self-directed reading is laudable, it is not enough for the librarian to keep abreast of his field. The author recommends that library schools take on the responsibility of organizing courses up to six months in duration to up-date librarians on current trends and problems. Librarians would have sabbatical leave to attend classes. Library schools could cover the whole field of librarianship or specialize by type of library. SELA and ALA should study ways of setting up programs for continued education.

77. Fryden, Floyd N. "Post-Master's Degree Programs in the

Accredited U.S. Library Schools." Library Quarterly.

39 (July 1969), 233-44.

The main focus of the article concerns formal programs of instruction (other than doctoral ones) at the post-master's degree level in 1967-68 and some of the problems which they raise.

The results are given of a questionnaire to the eleven library schools which offer such programs. Aspects discussed are the requirements for admission to a post-master's program; the stated objectives of the program; the nature of the curriculum to meet those objectives; the relation of the post-master's program to the doctorate; and starting date of program, enrollment, and number of Title II-B fellowships.

78. Galvin, Thomas J. The Case Method in Library Education

   and In-Service Training. Scarecrow, 1973. 288p.

   The author examines "the rationale of problem oriented
instruction as exemplified chiefly by the case method
approach in professional education." Librarianship has an
orientation toward the practical. Thus more emphasis is
placed on decision-making and problem solving as goals.
Arguments for and against the case method and related
teaching methods are presented. Four descriptive case
reports describe in detail the utilization of case studies
in an intensive media workshop; in teaching general and
school library administration, in general administration,
and use of the simulation method in teaching special library administration.

79. Gaver, Mary V. "The Educational Third Dimension:

   1. Continuing Education to Meet the Personalized

   Criteria of Librarians." Library Trends. 20 (July

   1971), 118-43.

   The above is a report of the results of a questionnaire examining the role of the individual professional
librarian in a plan for continuing education--his motivation, his criteria for such a program, and his strategies
for developing a course of lifelong learning. Since the
questionnaire was open ended, the responses are in essay
form. The evidence seems to indicate that many librarians
are participating in programs of external agencies, but
that there is a very definite need for a more organized
structure with the professional associations and the library schools sharing the major responsibility.

80. Gelinas, Jeanne. "Continuing Education for Library Staffs."

   Minnesota Libraries. 24 (Autumn 1973), 66-72.

Staff salaries account for 60 to 70 percent of most
annual operating budgets of libraries. Taxpayers have
the right to demand good service for this investment. One
of the articles in "The Library Rights of Adults: A Call
to Action" asserts that people have a right to library
staff "who recognize the value of continuing education for
themselves and their colleagues and who can train and in-
spire other staff." To develop staff, to continue one's
own learning and education, takes commitment, time, and
money. The author recommends that 1 percent of the library's budget be allocated to initiate a staff development program and have the staff involved in the planning
of the program's content.

81. Ginsburg, Eli and Brown, Carol A. Manpower for Library

Service. New York: Columbia University. 1967.

64p. ED 023 408.

The present state of library manpower and the outlook
for the future is assessed in terms of manpower analysis.
The field of library science is appraised within the
larger framework of such comparable fields as teaching,
social work, and nursing which also make use of large
numbers of female workers. Important findings and conclusions are: 1) the field of librarianship has responded
to expanded demands by rapidly increasing the number of
professional and para-professional workers; 2) the state
of preparation for the field is confused; 3) many graduate
programs, particularly doctoral, are weak; 4) it is
undesirable to establish a single set of standards for
manpower qualifications; 5) there is a need for more librarians to become acquainted with the new technology
for storage and retrieval; and 6) above all, the library
field needs to know more about its own human resources--
how they are recruited, trained, and utilized.

82. Goldstein, Harold. "The Importance of Newer Media in Li-

brary Training and the Education of Professional

Personnel." Library Trends. 16 (October 1967), 259-65.

Libraries devote little staff time to in-service training and formal audio-visual education programs for professional library personnel. Audio-visual equipment and materials are already obsolescent while commercial organizations make extensive use of well-designed training aids. More attention needs to be given to the acquisition, processing, storage, and retrieval of knowledge as distinguished from specific forms of library materials. Graduate library schools are the logical place to break the apathy and apprehension regarding new media. Regional groups could work cooperatively to set up orientation and training centers.

83. Goldstein, Harold. "Some Repetitious Points about In-

service Training for Audiovisual Services." Illinois

Libraries. 49 (Fall 1967), 118-21.

The effective implementation of audiovisual resources by librarians depends upon effective in-service training. The scope of the program must cover materials, equipment, services, and evaluation. The second item of importance in the scope of the training program is exposure to materials--previews, programs, practice with ideas about how to use materials. It is important that in-service training in this field be concerned with devising new services, since libraries have been mostly supply agencies for audiovisual materials without much original design of services peculiar to the library.

84. Goodrum, Charles A. "Are They Getting Their Money's Worth?

LC Assesses Fifteen Years of Its Special Recruit

Program." Library Journal. 91 (June 1, 1966), 2759-64.

The Library of Congress assesses fifteen years of its Special Recruit Program for outstanding graduates of library schools. Specific steps of the program are outlined. Statistical profiles are given of the 115 recruits. Of the 115 only 45 (39 percent) are still at LC. Survey results of both groups are given. LC has concluded that the recruiting program is worthwhile and will be continued.

85. Gregory, Ruth W. and Stoffel, Lester L. "Continuing Education for Librarianship." In: Public Libraries in Cooperative Systems; Administrative Patterns for Service. Chicago, American Library Association, 1971. 234-48.

Chapter 7 in this text is devoted to continuing professional education at the local, system and state level. The local level features in-service training programs; the second is a more detailed training program or refresher type of educational opportunity; and, the third is a research-based "new knowledge" educational program. Each level contributes to continuing education in terms of its own objectives, resources, and special competencies.

Ten general principles for continuing education programs are offered that are applicable at all three levels. Some are: the needs of participants must be clearly identified; the program must actively involve the participants; the program should be planned for continuous evaluation, etc.

The authors also provide an extensive outline of topics that are typical of continuing education efforts at the library system level.

86. Gutzman, Stanley D. "Career-long Sabbatical." Library Journal. 94 (October 1, 1969), 3411-15.

Too often in libraries, the only acceptable form of work for librarians is technical and administrative. Time taken during the day for intellectual pursuits is time stolen from the employer. However, the librarian "should

consider time spent at busy work as time wasted, and time
spent in intellectual pursuits, broadly defined, as time
used."

Administrators and librarians have the responsibility
to grow intellectually. Intellectual projects can be
both formal and informal, whether through some measured
output, such as an occasional article for publication,
or simply keeping abreast with the growing collection of
the library. The administrator needs to entrust his
staff with the responsibility that goes along with being
a professional and urge them to remain alert to developing discussion topics that would be of interest to other
members of the staff.

87. Hall, Anna C. <u>Selected Educational Objectives for Public</u>

<u>Service Librarians: A Taxonomic Approach</u>. Pitts-

burgh: University of Pittsburgh, 1968.

The goals of this study were to determine what skills
and knowledge were needed by librarians to implement
specific professional activities in large public libraries,
and to delineate the extent to which current library education developed those skills and knowledge. Librarians
in 13 large public libraries and faculty in 12 library
schools responded to the questionnaire. Their responses
were analyzed; a taxonomy was compiled of educational
objectives for the preparation of public service personnel.
The educational objectives were then analyzed and compared
with the curricular content of the participating library
schools.

Results show that: 1) librarians place a good deal
of importance on complex knowledges and skills; 2) library school curricula often do not include related
subject matter from other fields; 3) library schools
generally impart factual knowledge adequately; and 4) the
master's courses often neglect to impart the higher
intellectual skills above factual knowledge.

88. Hannigan, Jane A. "The Short Term Institute: A Vehicle

     for Continuing Education." School Media Quarterly.

     1 (Spring 1973), 193-97.

          A workshop builds on previously learned theory. It
     is short-range and impact-oriented in teaching specific
     skills. An institute, on the other hand, is theoretical
     in emphasis and only secondarily offers pragmatic applica-
     tions. An institute is a distinct and totally definable
     entity. The steps for designing, implementing, and
     evaluating an institute are given. The first step for an
     institute director is to select the thematic focus using
     five decisional criteria. Then he must set up behavioral
     goals and specific objectives. He must then consider
     the types of media to be used and personnel who will be
     involved. The environment of the institute is next
     considered--lodging for participants, meals, meeting
     rooms, and facilities for use of media. The selection
     of participants is the next crucial step. The audience
     should possess some degree of commonality in their back-
     ground and training and be of optimal size. Funding is
     also of critical importance in the selection of guest
     speakers, as well as publicity for the institute, adequate
     supportive staff, and the choice of a site. Lastly, a
     variety of evaluation techniques may be used during or
     after the institute to test whether the objectives have
     been met.

89. Harlow, Neal and others. Administration and Change:

     Continuing Education in Library Administration.

     New Brunswick, N.J.: Rutgers University Press, 1969.

     60p.

          The papers presented herein discuss the importance
     of continuing education for library administrators. Pro-
     fessional schools have two important effects upon library
     practice. The first is recruitment to the profession,

admission policies, and the preparation of people who are knowledgeable and responsive to change. The professional school's second means to influence the profession is through direct contact with administrators who make the decisions regarding curriculum.

The papers discuss the discipline of public administration with implications for library administration as well as the contributions of political science, sociology, and systems analysis to library administration.

90. Hart, T. L. and Jones, L. I. "Continuing Education:

Fact or Myth?" A pre-conference of the Indiana

Library Association. Focus. 24 (December 1970), 200-03.

91. Harvey, John F. and Lambert, Bettina. "The Educational

Third Dimension: II. Programs for Continuing Library Education." Library Trends. 20 (July 1971),

144-68.

There are many problems in keeping librarians up-to-date and continuing their education after their professional degree. The need for improving the current program of continuing education is described and specific recommendations are offered. A survey of types of programs is presented along with a list of "Fifteen Ideas for Dissemination."

92. Havens, S. "Midwinter for the Masses: A Report on a

'Program Without Precedent' at ALA Midwinter."

Library Journal. 92 (February 15, 1967), 738-42.

Summarized are the addresses of five speakers at the American Library Association's midwinter meeting. They are Cyril Houle, Margaret Monroe, Virginia McJenkin, Grace Stevenson and Fr. James Kortendick. They presented their observations on the general concepts, specific programs, and future needs of continuing education.

Professor Houle asserted that the professional association bears the chief collective responsibility for continuing education. Dr. Monroe outlined a statewide plan for continuing education which would entail four areas of learning; Ms. McJenkin recommended review and evaluation of continuing education programs for school librarians. Fr. Kortendick spoke on administration at the middle management level in libraries while Mrs. Stevenson commented on the need for coordination between informal workshops and formal education curricula to enable students to become proficient in subject areas.

93. Hempstead, John O. "Internship and Practical Application

in Educating School Library Personnel." Journal of

Education for Librarianship. 12 (Fall 1971), 116-32.

This article considers not only the place and form of practical application in library education, but also considers alternatives aimed at upgrading the library profession and providing for specialized needs emerging in the school library field.

Several aspects of internship are discussed: the components of an internship program; its purposes, goals, and objectives; definitions of internship, apprenticeship, and practicum; the need for internships and practical application in education and librarianship; results of internship programs; and implications for the preparation of school librarians.

94. Hershfield, Allan F. and Taylor, Robert S. <u>Library Educa-</u>

   <u>tion Redesign</u>. Education and Curriculum Series #1.

   School of Library Science. Syracuse University,

   1973. 87p.

   This is the first of a planned series of publications
   "intended to present fundamental studies in librarianship,
   in professional education for librarianship and information
   science, and in the design of curricula to meet emerging
   educational needs of a broad area called information
   transfer."

   The first article, "Effecting Change in Library Education" by Mr. Hershfield, suggests the need to change
   library education before change is brought about by outside forces. He points out the desirability of inter-
   disciplinary and multi-disciplinary approaches in library
   education programs, the need to attract different types
   of students into the profession. He also recommends that
   continuing education courses should be provided for library practitioners so that they too can acquire new
   knowledge and benefit from the results of research.

   The second article, "Curriculum Design for Library
   and Information Science" by Robert Taylor, states that
   library schools may need to extend their study programs
   beyond the traditional one-year Master's Degree program.

95. Hiatt, Peter. "Continuing Education." <u>College and Re-</u>

   <u>search Libraries</u>. 34 (March 1973), 101-02.

   Dr. Hiatt reports six major changes anticipated for
   post-secondary education in the next five to fifteen
   years based on the Delphi technique. Academic libraries
   must plan now to anticipate and redistribute their library resources and services through education: pre-
   service, formal, and continuing education. All levels
   of staff need to work together to meet client needs,
   formulate measurable objectives and evaluate their progress. Unfortunately, university libraries have failed
   to plan for the future and have relied on individual
   self-development.

96. Hiatt, Peter. "The Educational Third Dimension: III. Towa

the Development of Continuing Education for Library

Personnel." Library Trends. 20 (July 1971), 169-83.

The author argues that it is necessary to coordinate,
plan, stimulate, develop, and evaluate continuing education for library personnel, and that the responsibility
for doing so should rest with the professional associations at the national level. This article briefly reviews
the need for continuing education of all personnel working in libraries, discusses the elements which presently
contribute to our "system" of continuing education for
library personnel, and concludes that a national program
of continuing education is necessary. A description is
given of a model for a national program.

97. Hiatt, Peter. "WICHE [Western Interstate Commission for

Higher Education] Continuing Education Program for

Library Personnel." Illinois Libraries. 55 (May

1973), 332-36.

Mr. Hiatt is the director of the WICHE program which
was created in 1972. Its purpose is to identify the
continuing education needs of library personnel; develop
continuing education programs to meet those needs; to
evaluate those programs; and to seek outside funding to
build on core funding from the participating states.
With the exception of the Xerox Fund, WICHE was un-
successful in obtaining outside funding from library
oriented foundations or agencies. One agency did not
believe it was possible for a group of state library
agencies to work together successfully. The WICHE Western
Council on Continuing Education for Library Personnel is
now mounting several continuing education events in its
five member states: a three-day seminar on management-by-
objectives; verbal communications techniques for all types

of libraries, trustees, and lay leaders; and a slide/cassette
orientation for new public library trustees. WICHE can
initiate experimental programming and develop evaluative
techniques, materials, and results because it shares multi-
state resources, problems, and experiments.

98. Hines, Theodore C. <u>Programmed Learning and In-Service</u>

<u>Training in Libraries</u>. New York: Columbia University,

School of Library Service, n.d. (Mimeographed)

99. Hintz, Carl W. "The Librarian's Continuing Education."

<u>Pacific Northwest Library Association Quarterly</u>.

29 (January 1965), 120-22.

All professions experience not only obsolescence of
knowledge but the emergence of entire new fields of information. Librarians need not only keep up with the "basics"
of library science through continuing education but are
concerned with the newer fields of automation, documentation, and information retrieval.

Continuing education for librarians is compared with
that of the legal profession. The former is found almost
completely lacking in formal organization. The library
association is a logical source as the organizer of a
continuing education program on a formal basis and as a
normal part of the activities of the professional librarian.
Acceptance of such an idea is difficult because it requires the cooperation not only of the individual librarian
but also of his employer. Administrators need to inform
their professional staff that promotions and salary in-
creases will be based on participation in continuing education activities.

100. Horn, Andrew H. "Time for Decision: Library Education for

the Seventies." <u>Special Libraries</u>. 62 (December

1971), 515-23.

A model for a master's degree program in library and
information science is suggested. Degree requirements
should not be couched in terms of courses to be completed.
The degree ought to certify that its holder has presented
evidence of basic competencies needed for successful professional practice, and has also developed the basis for
a field of specialization. Professional associations
have a responsibility to define the competencies necessary
to practice at the professional level in the public
interest. Certification is needed to direct professional
education, and to make continuing education a necessity
rather than an option. Involvement of practitioners in
professional education is a dimension of continuing education. The possession of a master's degree in library
science does not mean the individual is a qualified librarian but has the groundwork on which he can begin his
career of continuing education. Library schools have been
unable to meet the demands for more continuing education
because they lack the funds, personnel, and other resources to provide the service. The author recommends
that there should be greater use of librarians as part-
time or temporary faculty members in library schools.
Conversely, library science faculty should be granted
leaves of absence to return to practice in the "real
world." The writer further suggests that there should be
a mix of students and professionals involved in workshops,
conferences, institutes, and meetings of professional
associations.

101. Houle, Cyril O. and Hiatt, Peter. "Continuing Education."

Michigan Librarian. 37 (Winter 1971), 21-22.

The nature of continuing education parallels the
readiness to change. Readiness for change and interest
in education for each professional involves four classes
or types: 1) the innovators, 2) the pace setters, 3) the
majority adapters, and 4) the laggards. Each type is
explained. Mr. Hiatt concludes that the best approach to
continuing education is through the library associations.

102. Indiana University, Graduate Library School, and Indiana

       State Library. "Public Library Service for the

       Inner-City Disadvantaged: A Title II-B Institute."

       In: Peter Hiatt and others. Education of State

       Library Personnel: A Report with Recommendations

       Relating to the Continuing Education of State Library

       Agency Professional Personnel. Chicago: American

       Library Association, 1971. pp. 37-45.

103. Jesse, Wm. H. and Mitchell, Ann E. "Professional Staff

       Opportunities for Study and Research." College and

       Research Libraries. 29 (March 1968), 87-100.

       Members of the teaching faculty are expected to spend
       part of their working time in study and research. This
       paper examines the extent of comparable opportunities
       available to academic librarians, as revealed by question-
       naires returned from fifty-two research libraries and
       fifteen college libraries. Among the opportunities con-
       sidered are time released from ordinary schedules for
       course work and research, sabbatical and special leaves
       for these purposes, and financial assistance. The extent
       of staff participation in study and research activities
       is presented, culminating in the discussion of a
       desirable library policy in this area.

104. Jones, Donna R. "Junior Members Round Table, Mountain-

       Plains Library Association, Speaks: An Interview."

       Mountain Plains Association Quarterly. 18 (Summer

       1973), 10-12.

In this question-answer format, the consensus of the Junior Members Round Table is given on professionalism and the need for continuing education. Some members feel they have been overtrained in some areas in library schools and have received too little training in public relations and middle management. Leadership development courses would help one learn to develop a sharing atmosphere among staff members. Perhaps library schools should consider intern work in a library with a practicing librarian.

105. Josey, E. J., and Blake, Fay M. "Educating the Academic

Librarian." Library Journal. 95 (January 15, 1970),

125-30.

The academic library has many new problems to face-- the publication explosion, technology, students who represent minorities, students involved in independent study programs, and user demand for unconventional materials. The librarian should have intensive study in an academic discipline leading toward a subject master's or a doctoral degree. He or she should also have a knowledge of research methods and an extensive background in languages. The academic librarian must view himself as an educator who can provide meaningful instruction in the use of the library rather than a brief tour of the facilities. The librarian needs to know about automation and the applications of it to his library. The library profession has accepted the premise that the individual librarian is primarily responsible for his continuing education once out of library school. However, other faculty members have ten-month contracts, sabbaticals, and access to grants. Academic librarians, many of whom have faculty status, should demand the same privileges. Library schools and academic libraries have a stake in providing continuing educational opportunities for their professional staff to insure quality library service.

106. Kaser, David E. "Continuing Education in the Library

      Profession." In: <u>Library Lectures; nos. 1-4</u>.

      Baton Rouge: Louisiana University, 1967.

      pp. 1-9.

      Self-education is necessary in combating the library
profession's tendencies to provincialism, conservatism,
insularism, and resistance to change. Very few libraries
maintain diligent internal programs of staff development.
Suggested are larger travel budgets to allow for attendance
at conferences, workshops, and trips to other libraries.

107. Kaser, David. "Making the Effort." In: Elizabeth W.

      Stone, ed. <u>New Directions in Staff Development</u>:

      <u>Moving from Ideas to Action</u>. Chicago: American Li-

      brary Association, Library Administration Division,

      1971. pp. 6-10.

      Continuing education in the library profession can be
viewed in several ways. Some see it as a management concern, others see it as the responsibility of the library
schools. Still others feel that ALA and other library
organizations should promulgate it. But the primary
requisite to success is the recognition by a majority of
librarians that they as individuals need continuing education and are willing to do the hard work required to
keep up with their profession.

108. Kaser, David. "The Training Subsystem." <u>Library Trends</u>.

      20 (July 1971), 71-77.

      The author is Director of the Cornell University Li-
braries. In 1970 he made a survey of 145 of the largest
libraries concerning their continuing education programs.
Although libraries are aware of the need for in-service
training of personnel, there is no systematic approach

being used. He describes the extent of library sources
that are being regularly budgeted for training and finds
them too low. Looking outside the field of library
science, the author illustrates the guidelines of a training subsystem proposed by the National Industrial Security
Association. He forecasts that libraries in the near
future will coordinate continuing education programs into
a single, institution-wide training module.

109. Kenney, Louis A. "Continuing Education for Academic Li-

brarians." California Librarian. 30 (July 1969),

199-202.

Academic librarians are working to gain faculty status
in California's academic community. Librarians desiring
parity with the faculty will have to produce comparable
scholarly qualifications and performance. Continuing education offers a partial remedy for this problem. Staffs
need released time from work to continue their professional advancement through individual study, formal and
informal education, research and publication. Library
schools should be preparing to give two or more years of
graduate training to persons entering the upper levels
of librarianship. Academic libraries will need to encourage librarians to participate in continuing education programs by providing incentive which would include
travel expenses and time away from the job without loss
of salary.

110. Klempner, I. M. "Information Centers and Continuing Edu-

cation for Librarianship." Special Libraries. 59

(November 1968), 729-32.

Two currently emerging information needs are those
for in depth information which frequently necessitates
detailed subject analysis and combinatory-type information
retrieval, and the need for critically-evaluated and
synthesized information. It is postulated that when the
need for particular services arises within our society,

society either obtains such services from existing institutions or creates new institutions to fulfill desired needs.
To satisfy the need for critically-evaluated and synthesized information, traditionally fulfilled on a part-time
basis by professionals within the respective subject
disciplines, society created and funded the information
center. To satisfy the demand for in depth information
service, a natural yet unfulfilled extension of library
service, society funded and also allocated this task to
the information center. The lack of continuing education
for librarians is considered to be a major factor con-
tributing to the inability of librarians, even special
librarians, to satisfy the newly emerging user demand
for in depth information.

111. Knox, Alan B. "Continuing Education for Library

Practitioners." Illinois Libraries. 56 (June 1974),

432-37.

Dr. Knox, Director of the Office of Continuing Education and Public Services, University of Illinois at
Urbana-Champaign, discusses the theoretical and philosophical aspects of continuing education for librarianship. He
notes that many library personnel are not aware of the
range of continuing education activities that are available to them, especially those programs sponsored by
associations and institutions of higher education. He
outlines and discusses six elements which comprise an
effective program of continuing education--context, needs,
objectives, activities, evaluation, and benefits. Listed
are three settings in which most continuing education
occurs: the individual, the temporary group, and the
organization. Advantages and disadvantages of each
setting are detailed. The author concludes that leadership is needed for effective programs of continuing education for librarianship to result.

112. Kortendick, James J. "Continuing Education and Library

     Administration." <u>ALA Bulletin</u>. 61 (March 1967),

     268-71.

     Graduates of library schools who find themselves in
supervisory positions quickly become aware of their own
shortcomings and the need for further education. Proposed are seminars to provide middle management with a
better understanding of their duties and responsibilities.
Top management in libraries, library school faculty, and
professional associations should cooperate in offering
these seminars.

113. Kortendick, James J. "Continuing Education for Librarians.

     In: Harold Borko, ed. <u>Targets for Research in Li-</u>

     <u>brary Education</u>. Chicago, American Library Associa-

     tion, 1973. pp. 145-72.

     Father Kortendick provides an historical review of
continuing library education, offers some tentative solutions for improvement, and cites specific research proposals. A bibliography is included.

114. Kortendick, James J. "Guide to Library Education. Part I:

     Curriculum: Administration." <u>Drexel Library Quarterl</u>

     3 (January 1967), 92-103.

     Father Kortendick cites trends in the teaching of li-
brary administration over the last forty years in graduate
library schools. He identifies several teaching techniques
which include field visits, role playing, case studies, etc

In the area of continuing education, administration
programs have been left to chance planning and sponsorship. Although certain libraries have developed a form
of in-service training for junior staff, there is little
available for those in middle management. The university
library school has many advantages as the locale for
long-range continuing education programs. Administrators
may need a year of professional education to learn new
tasks and master neglected fields, absorb new knowledge,
and interpret and deal with unfamiliar and new uncertainties.

115. Kortendick, James J.   "Research Needs in the Field of

Continuing Education for Librarians." In: Harold

Borko, ed. A Study of the Needs for Research in

Library and Information Science Education. Final

Report. Chicago: American Library Association,

1973. pp. 197-233.

The author presents eleven suggestions for research
proposals in continuing education. The first research
project proposed is a feasibility study of a national program of continuing education for librarians based on the
cooperative partnership of all agencies in the profession.
Other studies suggested all flow from or are part of this
general plan, such as: a national survey of needs; a study
of motivational factors related to continuing education;
and the development of effective communication and research
information exchange in library science. Four projects
take particular recognition of the importance of a systems
approach in the teaching-learning process combined with
the use of multi-media: 1) an evaluation of the abilities
of various media in meeting continuing education needs;
2) the development of packaged programs of study; 3) the
development of a model for staff development programs; and
4) a model for planning, implementation, and evaluation
of institutes. Three projects designed to meet special

needs of mid-career librarians are: 1) an exploratory
study of the advantages of closer relationships between
professors of library administration and library administrators; 2) an investigation of postgraduate internships; and 3) a study of the participation of librarians
in community affairs as a means of developing social
responsibility and professional growth.

116. Kortendick, James J. and Stone, Elizabeth W. "Education

Needs of Federal Librarians." Drexel Library Quarterl

6 (July-October 1970), 264-78.

This is a survey of post-M.L.S. needs as expressed by
federal librarians. Most respondents favored the workshop format and indicated high priority courses in the
areas of specialized library functions, automation, and
administration.

117. Kortendick, James J. and Stone, Elizabeth W. Job Dimen-

sions and Educational Needs in Librarianship. Chicago

American Library Association, 1971. 503p.

The project undertaken by the authors is a study of
the training of library personnel, especially at the
middle and upper levels. The rise to a higher level of
required skills and competencies--often new--has brought
about an urgent need for improved training beyond the
first professional degree at the post-master's level. To
establish a sound base for curriculum development, the
authors determine what concepts, knowledge, and techniques for middle and upper-level library personnel would
be needed to perform at an optimum level of efficiency.

118. Kortendick, James J. and Stone, Elizabeth W. Post-Master's

       Education for Middle and Upper Level Personnel in

       Libraries and Information Centers. Final Report,

       Phase I. Catholic University of America, Department

       of Library Science, 1970. 542p. ED 038 985.

A post-master's education program is an important
step in upgrading the profession of librarianship. The
above titled program used two data-gathering instruments
to develop the data base for the curriculum. The first
was a questionnaire; the second, interviews. The data are
given under three categories: questionnaire results,
interview results, and summary, conclusions and recommendations for further study. The main conclusions are: 1) an
interdisciplinary approach is needed for the program;
2) for planning and implementing the program, a systems
format should be used; 3) the orientation should be
practical and based in the library school; 4) the program
should include multi-media instruction; 5) motivational
factors should be incorporated; and 6) the program should
be available on a part-time basis for financial reasons.
Phase I includes numerous graphs and tables illustrating
the findings.

119. Kortendick, James J. and Stone, Elizabeth W. Post-Master's

       Education for Middle and Upper Level Personnel in

       Libraries and Information Centers. Final Report,

       Phase II. Project No. 8-0731. Washington, D.C.:

       Office of Education, Department of Health, Education,

       and Welfare, 1972. Included with the final report are

       three packaged Post-MLS courses edited by Rev. James J.

       Kortendick, S.S., and Elizabeth W. Stone. Becker,

       Goodman, and Zachert author each of the three courses.

120.   Kronick, David A., Rees, Alan M., and Rothenberg, L.   An

       Investigation of the Educational Needs of Health

       Sciences Library Manpower: Part VII: Summary and Con

       clusions.   Cleveland: Case Western Reserve Univer-

       sity, 1970.   22p.

121.   Kronus, Carol.   "Inducing Attitudinal Change Among Libraria

       Journal of Education for Librarianship.   12 (Fall 197)

       104-15.

           Thirty-five librarians who participated in a training
       program on library service to the inner city were surveyed
       concerning their attitudes before and after a five-day
       conference. A control group of thirty public librarians
       in similar administrative positions and size of library
       were randomly selected. The semantic differential was
       used with both groups. The participating librarians
       showed statistically significant changes in their atti-
       tudes as a result of the conference. The concepts that
       underwent change were The Urban Poor, Community Involve-
       ment in Planning Library Programs, and Library Institutes
       as Educational Devices. Post-test scores of both groups
       showed that participants moved in the opposite direction
       from the expressed attitudes of the control group. The
       article discusses the implications of this study and
       offers two theories concerning attitude change in
       conference formats.

122.   Kutztown State College Department of Library Science.

       Educational Trends: Innovations, Technology, Multi-

       Media, Taxonomies of Learning, Librarianship: A

       Bibliographical Checklist, 1965-1971.   Kutztown, Pa.:

       Kutztown State College, 1971.

123. Ladendorf, Janice M. <u>The Changing Role of the Special Li-</u>

<u>brarian in Industry, Business, and Government</u>. SLA

State-of-the-Art Review, no. 1. New York: Special

Libraries Association, 1973. 29p.

The special librarian finds his role changing with
the increase in the information explosion. Users require
an increasing variety in forms of information. Although
the librarian's service goals remain the same, new
techniques have evolved to keep up with the flood of published literature. Two examples of this are information
science and networking. Information science offers the
technique of the computer and management analysis. More
research is needed on the special librarian's role. For
example, one area that needs further exploration is the
problem of evaluating services from the user's point of
view.

124. Lee, Robert E., Allen, Lawrence A., and Hiatt, Peter.

<u>A Plan for Developing a Regional Program of Continuing</u>

<u>Education for Library Personnel in the Western States</u>.

Boulder, Colorado: Western Interstate Commission

for Higher Education, 1969. 66p. ED 047 767.

The Western Interstate Commission for Higher Education (WICHE) is working with its member states to develop
a long-range continuing education program for library
personnel. WICHE is using several educational methods to
develop an integrated program for library personnel. The
proposed four-year plan has four periods: 1) a transitional
stage to recruit and train program associates; 2) phase
one, in which the program director will establish organizational structure and supportive activities; 3) phase two,
in which there is state level staff and a program with a
State Director in each state concomitant with continuing
regional educational activities; and 4) evaluation to
determine the impact of program and plans for the future.

125.   Liesener, James W.   "The Development of a Planning Process

for Media Programs."   School Media Quarterly.

(Summer 1973), 278-87.

Herein is a summary of a conceptual framework and
processes for media program planning. Discussed are the
requirements of media program management tools and a
media program model. The planning process involves nine
steps: 1) definition of program output alternatives;
2) survey of perceptions of current services; 3) determination of service preferences and priorities in relation
to local needs; 4) assessment of resource and operational
requirements of services; 5) determination of costs of
preferred services and/or current services; 6) calculation
of program capability; 7) communication of preferred
services currently feasible to total client group; 8) re-
allocation of resources and implementation of changes in
operations to provide the range and level of services
selected; and 9) periodic evaluation of services offered
and documentation of changing needs. While planning of
this nature requires considerable time and staff involvement, accountability requires that the best use of resources be made to provide maximum service to all.

126.   Lindsey, Elizabeth.   "Continuing Education in Michigan."

Illinois Libraries.   56 (June 1974), 459-62.

Michigan has focused on continuing education for professionals and nonprofessionals in a variety of settings.
Workshops sponsored by the State Library, universities,
community colleges and library associations have covered
current topics of interest. Specific workshops are cited.
One of the weaknesses in continuing education is that
clerical staff receive little ongoing training. Not
everyone takes advantage of the organizational library
activities. The same people appear for workshops while
others who could profit from such experiences either
cannot get away from their jobs or lack the motivation to
attend. The workshops in Michigan have presented a wide

range of topics: the library's role in American Indian
education; how to effect outreach service to those in
correctional institutions, hospitals, and schools to the
emotionally disturbed; the problems of censorship; lack
of funds; and, service to the blind. Human Development
Through Reading concentrated on selection of materials for
use in therapeutic service to alert librarians to those
least served.

127. Lowther, Barbara A. "Lincoln Open University--Bringing

College to the Library." Illinois Libraries. 56

(June 1974), 439-41.

Lincoln Open University is a private institution
established in 1973 to serve the people of Illinois and
Indiana. It has degree-granting authority through the
master's degree. It has no campus and does not offer
courses of study but works through a consortium of existing academic institutions and community learning resources to help a student plan his own course of study.
Adults 25 years of age or more are the primary participants. Students pursue individual programs in "study
centers" established primarily in public libraries.

128. Martin, Allie Beth. "Continuing Library Education

What's Happening? Who's Responsible?" Illinois

Libraries. 56 (June 1974), 437-39.

Mrs. Martin contributes a model for a coordinated
program for all library personnel which involves all
relevant agencies and organizations. The model is a
general outline of the purposes, goals, and allocation
of responsibility for planning a continuing education
program.

129. Martin, Allie Beth. "Out of the Ivory Tower." Library

Journal. 96 (June 15, 1971), 2060.

Four elements are suggested for the successful implementation of continuing education: 1) a mix of full-time
academicians and part-time faculty who are actively participating in libraries; 2) content and presentation that
deal with current problems, trends, and needs of the
participants using various kinds of media; 3) participants
at all levels of employment should be included with
formal recognition given for achievement; and 4) funding
should be supported by library associations at all levels
as well as Federal funds for experimental programs.

130. Martin, Allie Beth. A Strategy for Public Library Change;

Proposed Public Library Goals--Feasibility Study.

Chicago: American Library Association, 1972.

131. Martin, Allie Beth, and Duggan, Maryann. Continuing Edu-

cation for Librarians in the Southwest: A Survey

and Recommendations. Dallas, Texas: Southwestern

Library Association, 1973.

The Southwestern Library Association is firmly committed to a leadership role in developing a program of
continuing education for library personnel in its six
member states. The purpose of the Continuing Education
for Library Staffs in the Southwest (CELS) project was
to assess continuing education of library staffs in the
six states and to propose a plan of action designed to
meet the needs of the region as perceived from a study
and survey. A questionnaire was sent to all components
of the profession responsible for continuing education:
individual libraries, library schools, library associations, and state library agencies. Results showed
limited continuing education opportunities throughout the
region. Strategy groups representing national library
leaders, library schools, etc., made a series of recommendations included in this report. The major recommendation resulting from this study is that the Southwestern Library Association assume the responsibility of

developing and coordinating a viable continuing education
program with other library agencies in the region.

132. McCarthy, Dorothy R. "Impact of HEA Title II-B Institutes
in Librarianship." In: The Florida State University.
School of Library Science, Leadership Training
Institute. Palo Alto, California: CSC/Pacific, 1973.

   This report is the result of a survey of the narrative
evaluations of fifty institutes for training in librarianship during the years 1968-1972 when federal support of
library training was at its peak. A good deal of information is provided on the educational features of in-
stitutes--the logistics involved in scheduling, length of
programs; summer short-term vs. academic year institutes,
patterns of library cooperation, and conclusions and
recommendations. The author concludes that short-term
institutes designed for target groups who share a common
purpose are most successful.

133. McDonough, Roger H. Library Education in New Jersey.
Report and Recommendations of a Study Sponsored by
the New Jersey Department of Higher Education and the
New Jersey Department of Education. Conducted by
the New Jersey State Library with the assistance of
an Advisory Committee. Trenton, N.J.: New Jersey
State Library, 1972. 46p.

   As one of its recommendations for immediate action,
the New Jersey State Library recommends that continuing
education for all levels of library staff be encouraged
and not expected to be self-supporting since the State
Library and Rutgers Graduate School of Library Service

recognize their responsibility to update professional
training. The graduate level extension course program
sponsors continuing education. The State Library, professional associations, and educational institutions
will coordinate programs to meet the continuing education
needs of librarians. Courses will deal with specialized
knowledge geared toward improved performance, promotion,
and personal development.

Also included is a summary of findings of library
manpower patterns and projections in New Jersey. On
continuing education, library directors responded as
follows: 1) school librarians and college library
directors were more favorable toward continuing education
than were public library directors; 2) the higher the
school level at which the librarian worked and the higher
the certification level of the librarian, the more likely
he was in favor of continuing education; 3) college librarians had the highest participation in continuing education, next highest were special library directors, and
lowest were public library directors; and 4) released time
was available for staff members to attend in-service and
continuing education programs.

134. McGlothlin, W. J. "Continuing Education in the Professions

Journal of Education for Librarianship. 13 (Summer

1972), 3-16.

The author presents a capsule review of the concepts
and practices used in continuing education by professions
other than librarianship. Associations of every profession hold technical conferences, publish journals, make
studies, and generally attempt to stimulate the professiona
growth of their members. An agency is conceived of as a
"learning community" rather than merely as an "administrative community." As a final way of stimulating continuing
education, some states have enacted statutes or regulations
to require each member of the profession to undertake some
kind of educational activity at stated levels, e.g.,
teachers, dentists.

135. McJenkin, Virginia. "Continuing Education for School Li-

brarians." <u>ALA Bulletin</u>. 61 (March 1967), 272-75.

The rapid development of school libraries and the
changing patterns of school library organization and service
demand a review and evaluation of present programs of continuing education and also demand long-range plans for
effectively serving the needs of various levels of school
library personnel. Those responsible for providing continuing education opportunities are the state departments
of education and local school systems, professional library associations, and library schools and other institutions offering courses. There is a notable increase
in the areas for which continuing education experiences
are being provided. Both formal and informal education
programs are cited and a list of continuing needs for
school librarians is given.

136. McNamee, Gil W. "Staff Development." <u>Synergy</u>. 33

(Summer 1971), 35-37.

The (San Francisco) Bay Area Reference Center (BARC)
has an on-going continuing education program. BARC has
presented twenty-two workshops to libraries of the North
Bay Cooperative Library System; seven other systems are
also participating. BARC experiments with all types of
audio-visual aids and demonstrates their use to librarians.
A relatively small amount of money can support a permanent,
well planned continuing education program.

Some of the weaknesses of other in-service training
approaches are discussed. One popular misconception is
that the only training one needs is actual work experience. Others rely on general or departmental training
but these are isolated and do not build on previous
discussions. Some librarians believe that keeping abreast
of the profession by reading library literature is
sufficient. While others believe that membership in
professional organizations is an excellent means of education.

137. Medical Library Association. Director of Medical Library

Education. Questionnaire on Continuing Education,

August, 1973. Chicago: Medical Library Association,

1973.

The Medical Library Association was interested in
surveying the continuing education needs of medical librarians. The above is a questionnaire developed for
that purpose.

138. Meyer, R. S. "Library Schools for Special Librarians:

Commentary." Sci-Tech News. 27 (Fall 1973), 82-84.

139. Meyer, Ursula. "New York's Statewide Continuing Profes-

sional Education Program: The Early Stages of Develop-

ment." Paper presented at the First Annual Staff

Development Micro-Workshop, American Library Associa-

tion Convention, Detroit, Michigan, June 28, 1970.

In: Elizabeth W. Stone, ed. New Directions in

Staff Development: Moving from Ideas to Action.

Chicago: American Library Association, 1971. 16-27.

New York State is developing a long-range approach to
continuing education geared toward the professional (post-
library degree) level librarian. It is coordinated by the
Division of Library Development. Seven objectives for a
statewide continuing education program are outlined by the

New York State Department of Education. To encourage participation in the planned program, questionnaires were
sent to the Public Library Systems and their members to
determine the areas of need for continuing education.
The results of the questionnaires and personal interviews
are summarized. The patterns of responses fall into a
general pattern: the necessity for continuing professional
education, released time to attend the sessions, planning
for program content and approach, training of community
(paraprofessional) librarians, the role of other agencies,
and so on. The Appendix lists the specific questions
that comprise the personal interview form.

140. Midwest Regional Continuing Education Meeting. Depart-

ment of Library Science. Wayne State University,

November 5, 1971, 6p.

Representatives of midwest state libraries, state library associations, and ALA-accredited library schools were
invited by Wayne State University to discuss the feasibility
of a long-range, regional program of continuing education
for librarians in all types of libraries. This report
summarizes the findings offered by the participants.

141. Monroe, Margaret E. "Variety in Continuing Education."

ALA Bulletin. 61 (March 1967), 275-78.

The first task of continuing education should be that
of reducing the resistance to change. A statewide plan
for continuing education for librarians will require
attention to four aspects: foundation, remedial, emergency,
and specialization of learning. If librarianship is viewed
as professional group practice, then each librarian has
a specific area in which he plans, carries out, and
evaluates his program, for which he continuously perfects
his professional capacity, and in which he makes his professional contribution.

142. "National Planning Urged for Continuing Education."

     Library Journal. 97 (February 1, 1972), 444+.

     The American Library Association submitted its recom-
     mendations on The Education of State Library Personnel.
     It encourages an initial program to train one staff
     member from each state library agency in consulting
     skills and on participative laboratory methods of adult
     learning. These persons, after five days training by
     the Western Interstate Commission for Higher Education
     Program for Library Personnel, would then return to their
     agencies to act as coordinators of continuing education
     for state library personnel. Also recommended is a
     National Advisory and Action Committee for Continuing
     Education of State Library Personnel. This would meet
     twice a year and serve as the prototype for a similar
     body charged with overseeing all continuing education
     for librarianship.

143. Navarre, C. "Decision Flowcharts as Training Tools in

     Libraries." Information: Part 2. 1 (July 1972), i-1

144. Neufeld, John. [letter]. Journal of Education for

     Librarianship. 6 (Fall 1965), 144-47.

     In proposing any program of continuing education for
     librarians, the author is concerned that bureaucratic
     controls will be superimposed on the profession so that
     the specter of compulsory or quasi-compulsory adult edu-
     cation for the librarian will result. Since the librarian
     has graduated from a formal library school program he has
     learned the means to find the information he wants.

145. "New Western Reserve Program Plans Continuing Education

     (for Medical Librarians)." Library Journal. 92

     (June 15, 1967), 2341.

The School of Library Science at Western Reserve began
an experimental program to identify aspects of library
practice most subject to obsolescence and developed a means
for evaluating the effectiveness of alternate approaches
to providing continuing education.

146. New York State Education Department. New York State

Library. "New York Libraries Agree on New Focus:

The Adult Independent Learner." The Bookmark. 33

(January-February 1974), 70-75.

The results of a conference on the adult independent
learner are listed. The seventy representatives at the
meeting are from New York State public libraries and
public library systems, and State and Federal education
agencies. Their consensus is that the public library
has the special responsibility of working with the adult
learner who chooses to remain independent of a formal
educational program. After listing some of the types of
services presently provided in libraries throughout New York
State, the Task Force outlines the goals and objectives
for implementing a continuing education program, the staff
training that will be needed, publicity, and resources
that will need to be utilized.

Public library services to the adult independent
learner would involve three steps: 1) individual contact between the librarian and the learner; 2) group activities with other independent learners to share learning
and experiences; and 3) liaison with all community organizations and other library agencies offering similar
services.

147. Nyren, Karl. "Threats to Professionalism." Library

Journal. 99 (October 1, 1974), 2425.

This is an LJ editorial concerning the growing threat to the present status of "The Librarian." Some of the "threats" are automation of library processes, increase of clerical workers to handle routine work and "credit for experience" work incentive programs. One of several solutions recommended is that library schools and associations encourage continuing education programs because library science has its own unique discipline which must be preserved.

148. Office for Library Personnel Resources (OLPR) Bulletin.

American Library Association. 1 (May 1974).

This is the first issue of a quarterly which will deal with some aspect of recruitment to the library profession, library science education, or personnel as a feature article. As regular features in each issue it will have a staff development bibliography and a directory of continuing education workshops and institutes.

149. O'Loughlin, Sister Anne J. "Catholic Library Association's

Commitment to Continuing Education." Catholic

Library World. (November 1970), 185-87.

The Catholic Library Association amended its Constitution to extend its membership to all librarians for the purpose of encouraging cooperation among national, state, and local library associations. This is a general article that deals with the broad goals of the Catholic Library Association.

150. Osborn, Jeanne. "Innovation in Library Education." Librar

Journal. 98 (November 15, 1973), 3341-50.

Taking into account the recommendations in the Carnegi Commission Report on Higher Education, this paper examines recent landmark documents on library education, particularly the 1970 ALA statement on Library Education and

Manpower and to a lesser degree, the 1972 Committee
on Accreditation Standards for graduate programs
leading to the first professional degree. Although the
Carnegie report is general, it challenges some traditional policies of library schools in regard to admission, curriculum, and certification.

Also included as an addendum to the paper are the
reaction of several library school educators. They are:
Ralph Blasingame, Martha Boaz, George Bobinski, Margaret
Chisholm, Guy Garrison, Norman Horrocks, Jean Lowrie,
Kenneth Shaffer, Roy Stokes, and William Summers.

151. Paullin, Alyce Klussman. "Participation, Learning

Achievement, and Perceived Benefit in a Televised

Continuing Medical Education Program." Unpublished

doctoral dissertation, The Catholic University of

America, 1971.

152. Peck, Theodore P. "Continuing Education and the Academic

Librarian." Mn U Bulletin. 3 (October 1972), 111-16.

There is a trend for school librarians to become
media generalists not only in name but also because of
additional training in audiovisual technology. Academic
librarians as well are showing interest in converting
their libraries into learning resource centers. In a few
institutions academic librarians are working with faculty
in designing curricula not only in the use of libraries
and literature, but in other fields as well. Four
approaches are recommended for continuing education:
1) enroll in an introductory or general type course--com-
puter operations, the use of audiovisual equipment,
principles of learning, and so on; 2) develop an acquaint-
ance with the literature in related fields of AV,
education, information science; 3) join professional
associations; and 4) make on-site visits to exemplary
media resource centers.

153. Penland, Patrick R. <u>Advisory Counseling for Librarians</u>.

Pittsburgh, Pennsylvania: Graduate School of Library

and Information Sciences, University of Pittsburgh,

1970. 179p.

There is little in library literature concerning
training in interpersonal communications. This publication deals with the communications aspects of advisory
service to adults and the training needs of librarians
doing advisory work. The papers presented herein provide
a methodology for interviewing, guidance, counseling, and
interpersonal communications. It is hoped that these
techniques will help adult services librarians overcome
lack of ability or insecurity in helping the patron identi
his purposes and interests.

154. Penland, Patrick R. <u>Media Designed Programs for Librarian</u>

Pittsburgh, Pennsylvania: Graduate School of Library

and Information Science, University of Pittsburgh,

1970. 54p.

The purpose of this manual is to enable librarians to
help readers use a variety of media. Librarians themselves may feel uncomfortable with media integrated programs. The author discusses elements of programming,
production planning, program production, and graphics
preparation. He presents a practical rather than a
theoretical approach.

155. "Personnel: New Duties, New Training." <u>Wisconsin Library</u>

<u>Bulletin</u>. 65 (September - October, 1969), 347-72.

The greater part of this issue is devoted to the
training of library personnel. Nine articles on the subject cover the areas of: 1) recruitment, 2) the implications of the new media on personnel, 3) the training of
media-support people, 4) the relationship between the
Coordinating Council for Higher Education on libraries
and library education, 5) the Oshkosh (Wisconsin) Graduate
Library School program training for library technical
assistants, 6) criteria for programs to prepare library
technical assistants, 7) training for library technical
assistants, 8) Wisconsin school libraries in the National
Manpower Study, and 9) need for media training.

156.   "Personnel Training Workshop Explains Objectives of Program."

Kansas Library Bulletin. 41 (1972), 22.

Kansas has a statewide Personnel Development Project
aimed toward library personnel at four levels--from librarians who have a high school diploma to those with
graduate degrees in library science and professional
experience. Each system is responsible for at least eight
workshops during the year. Topics to be covered statewide are story-telling, budget preparation, community
survey, filing, and two reference sessions.

157.   Phillips, Kathleen. "Training for Federal Librarians."

Federal Library Committee Newsletter. 22 (June

1968), 7-13.

The U.S. Civil Service Commission's Bureau of Training made a survey of Federal librarians in all parts of
the United States and territorial possessions. Questions
dealt with personal characteristics, Federal library
experience, recency and types of training, and views concerning needs in the field of training which the librarians recognize as presently unfulfilled. The findings
are summarized in this article. The author concludes that
three groups share responsibility for keeping aware of

new developments in the field of library science: the
first responsibility must be assumed by the librarian in
terms of self-development; the second responsibility
belongs to the library managers in each agency to provide
leadership and guidance; and the third responsibility
rests with professional societies. The author offers
several examples of action that the Federal Library Committee or another similar group could take to assume a
leadership role in continuing professional education.

158.   Polette, Nancy. <u>In-Service: School Library/Media Work-</u>

        <u>shops and Conferences</u>. Scarecrow Press, 1973. 313p.

        This unique book covers the complete planning, execu-
tion, and topics of in-service workshops. The author
lists the steps to be taken for library staff to make an
instructional media survey. She then analyzes media programs that have been presented in school districts
throughout the country. A section of the book is devoted
to the training of paraprofessionals (library aides,
volunteers). Their duties are outlined. Sample letters,
programs, orientation sessions, and detailed "how to"
lessons are included as teaching devices. Every possible
facet of conference planning is included. Examples of
past conferences--local, state, and national--are presented
The last chapter concerns college and university programs.
Actual case studies of problems encountered in using media
materials and facilities are included.

159.   Portteus, Elnora M. "Staff Development: Reassessing."

        <u>School Media Quarterly</u>. 1 (Spring 1973), 213.

        The author, President of the American Association of
School Librarians, urges an on-going program for staff
development in media centers involving professionals, paraprofessionals, technical clerks, student aids, and volunteer

Sporadic in-service courses are giving way to increased
specialization among staff who are uniquely trained at
ever increasing competencies. Several general questions
are posed for the individual who is responsible for
planning continuing education at the building level,
system, or district level.

160.   Prentice, Anne E. The Public Library Trustee: Role Per-

ception in Relation to Performance in Obtaining

Funds for the Medium-Sized Library. D.L.S. thesis,

Columbia University, 1972. Ann Arbor, Michigan,

Xerox Microfilms, 1973.

161.   Presthus, Robert. Technological Change and Occupational

Response: A Study of Librarians. Final Report.

Part of the Maryland Manpower Research Program.

Washington, D.C.: U.S. Office of Education, 1970.

141p. ED 045 129.

Librarianship is undergoing change as it moves toward
unionization and professionalization. Automation and
reorientation toward working-class clientele and ethnic
groups are removing librarianship from its traditional
role. Five areas covered in this text are social change
and organizational accommodation, organizational and
authority structure, social and occupational values, and
potential for accommodation.

162.   "Project to Study Medical Librarianship." Library of

Congress Information Bulletin. 26 (May 18, 1967), 320.

Western Reserve University has a research grant from
the U.S. Public Health Service to conduct a one-year
experimental program in continuing education for medical
librarians. Alan Rees and Robert Sheshier will direct
the project which will have three parts: 1) review of
the present state of library practice in terms of formal
training and experience of regional medical librarians,
their study habits and work patterns; 2) short courses
in areas of professional competence; and 3) evaluation of
the courses.

163.   Radford, N.J. FLC Symposium on Important Study titled,

Post-Master's Education for Middle and Upper-Level

Personnel in Library and Information Centers.

Library of Congress Information Bulletin. 29

(November 5, 1970), 593-95.

Rev. James Kortendick, Director of the Department of
Library Science at Catholic University spoke to members
of the Federal Library Committee (FLC) at the Library of
Congress regarding the above titled study. Father Kortend
outlined the background and objectives of the entire project, and then reviewed the methodology used in Phase I,
the first of this three part project completed. The high
points of the information gathered from Phase I are summarized. Recommendations for further research based on
the findings are listed in six points.

164.   "Ralph Conant--In Pursuit of Library Education." American

Libraries. 4 (December 1973), 663.

Ralph Conant is director of the Southwest Center for
Urban Research in Houston. Although not a librarian,
Conant has a special interest in library education, having
served on the advisory committee to ALA's Office for Library Education. He is now involved in a library education study with Kathleen Molz. Conant feels that

librarians need more continuing education. More linkage
is needed between training in library schools and its
relevance to the problems of librarians in the field.

165. Reed, Sarah R. "Guide to Library Education. Part 1:

   Trends in Professional Education." Drexel Library

   Quarterly. 3 (January 1967), 1-24.

   Trends in professional education in several fields
are given with an emphasis on librarianship. Trends are
noted in administrative organization, admissions, other
student affairs, faculty, curriculum, research, finance,
and accreditation. While pre-service education may be
the usual entry into a profession, continuing education
is not only the means to advancement but to maintaining
respectability and competence. Only through programs of
continuing education can librarians keep abreast of new
knowledge and practice.

   Several broad recommendations are offered for professional library education--the need for long-range
planning; encouragement of keeping vital inter-disciplinary
relationships and relationships between teaching and research; the setting up of appropriate training programs
for each level of support staff; and the maintenance of
a continuing review of educational goals and programs in
relation to the community served.

166. Reed, Sarah R., ed. Problems of Library School Administra-

   tion: Report of an Institute, April 14-15, 1965,

   Washington, D.C. Washington, D.C.: U.S. Dept. of

   Health, Education and Welfare, 1965. 71p.

   This publication presents the papers prepared for the
Institute on Problems of Library School Administration.
Topics covered are problems of faculty, curriculum, and
finance; trends and problems of higher education and
accreditation; and current legislation with implications

for library education and an outline of a Library Services
Branch program for library education. Specifically,
Raynard C. Swank speaks on the graduate library school
curriculum while Paxton Price discusses legislation
relating to library education.

167. Rees, Alan, and others. Education for Hospital Library

Personnel: Feasibility Study for Continuing Educa-

tion of Medical Librarians. Interim Report no. 1.

Cleveland, Ohio: Case Western Reserve University,

1968. 70p. ED 027 931.

The hospital library is an integral part of the
national and regional medical library networks. These
libraries need to be upgraded to fully participate in
these networks.

The purpose of this study is to design, implement,
and evaluate educational offerings for hospital library
personnel. The research will provide a data bank concerning the location, resources, facilities, functions,
budget, services, and personnel of all hospital libraries
in Ohio. The dynamics of hospital-library relationships
is also studied. The education of hospital librarians
and the modification of the attitude of other library
personnel towards libraries in the hospital environment
also need upgrading.

168. Rees, Alan and Rothenberg, L. "An Investigation of the

Educational Needs of Health Sciences Library Manpower

Characteristics of Manpower in the Health Sciences

Libraries." Bulletin of the Medical Library

Association. 59 (January 1971), 31-40.

A mail survey was made of personnel in 2,099 health
sciences libraries located in other than hospital settings.
Respondents fell into three groups: professionals (those
having a graduate library degree), nonprofessionals (those
not having a library degree) and chief librarians (those
in charge of a library's operations). Results are
reported on sex, age, education, salary, job mobility,
and attitudes concerning continuing education programs.
Professionals preferred courses concerning the organization of libraries and health science institutions. Nonprofessionals were more interested in programs in technical
processing.

169. Rees, Alan M. and Rothenburg, L. "Analysis of the Demo-

graphic, Educational, and Employment Characteristics

of Participants in the Continuing Education Program

of the Medical Library Association." Bulletin of

the Medical Library Association. 58 (April 1970),

159-62.

A survey of the participants in the Continuing Education Program of the MLA reveals that most are college
graduates with fifty percent holding library degrees.
The population shows a high degree of geographic and job
stability. Most participants hold positions which require supervision of several employees.

170. "Report of the Committee on Seminar and Institute Topics."

Journal of Library Automation. 6 (September 1973),

139-44.

The Information Science and Automation Division (ISAD)
of the American Library Association appointed an ad hoc
committee to propose a plan for a program of institutes
and seminars within the interests and educational needs
of ISAD. The plan would cover the years 1974 to 1978.

A review of the historical data about ISAD seminars and institutes is discussed followed by a series of recommendations based on the consensus of the committee within the framework of the stated objectives of ISAD. The committee found three major problem areas in institutes: subject weakness in institute speakers, misplaced expectations, and participant heterogenity.

171. Ridge, Davey-Jo S. "Fie on Thee, Dr. Allen! A Reply to

L. A. Allen's Philosophy of Library Education."

South Carolina Librarian. 14 (March 1970), 21-23.

Dr. Lawrence Allen of the School of Library Science at the University of Kentucky suggested that the history of books and the foundations of librarianship be taught at the undergraduate level and that cataloging and reference be taught on the job. A graduate degree in library science should consist of courses in the behavioral sciences. Mrs. Ridge refutes Dr. Allen's thesis, stating that the librarian's main goal is to furnish information and materials to patrons not to analyze the patron who needs it. There are three reasons why in-service training in reference and cataloging would be unworkable at least from the academic librarian's viewpoint. First, an experienced staff of superior quality would be necessary to work with an "apprentice." Few librarians would feel qualified to assume this responsibility or have the time free from their work schedule. Mediocre librarians would give inadequate instruction. Secondly, the quality and quantity of the book collection would place a limitation on the training, not only for reference but for cataloging Thirdly, this type of in-service training would be confined to a specific reference collection or to eccentricities of classification employed by a particular library. Dr. Allen's theory would obviate librarianship as a profession in which the principles of its practice require intensive academic preparation.

172. Rockwood, Ruth H. <u>Personnel Utilization in Libraries,</u>

<u>Selected Papers</u>. Tallahassee, Florida: Florida

State University School of Library Science, 1970.

ED 046 464.

The Florida State University School of Library
Science sponsored an institute on the utilization of
personnel in libraries. Papers presented at the institute cover three broad categories: 1) changing points of
view toward personnel administration; 2) steps in select-
ing candidates for middle management; and 3) ways and
means of developing effective leadership. Shortages of
library personnel exist at all levels, especially in
middle management positions. Libraries have not made
optimal use of their personnel.

Some of the Papers concern professional librarians
who have administrative responsibilities and management
experience. Suggestions are offered to make better use
of staffs to improve the library. Subjects discussed are:
1) leadership, 2) morale and democratic administration,
3) policy of selection, 4) communication, 5) civil service,
6) selective devices, 7) decision making and delegation
of authority, 8) opportunities for growth, 9) the management team, 10) a panel discussion on in-service training
and 11) a model for personnel utilization.

173. Rogers, A. Robert. "What's Your Score: Assessing a Li-

brary's Potential for Change." <u>Ohio Library Associa-</u>

<u>tion Bulletin</u>. 40 (January 1970), 11-12.

An approach to measure librarians' attitudes toward
change is presented. Although the measure is crude, the
scale has five major positions ranging from extreme
eagerness (radical) to extreme reluctance (reactionary).
The individual's self-perception of where he stands on

changes in library procedures is supplemented by the perceptions of those who see him in action. Members of the
staff can become aware of how others perceive their attitudes. Several questions are put forth on the usefulness
of this information--Which approach (radical, liberal,
moderate, conservative, reactionary) is most characteristic of the top administration? Of middle management?
If a deliberate choice is possible, which approach would
be preferable in problem solving?

174. Rothstein, Samuel. "Nobody's Baby: A Brief Sermon on

Continuing Professional Education." _Library Journal_.

90 (May 15, 1965), 2226-227.

While librarianship offers a variety of continuing
education programs, the duplication of programming is
evident and the coverage of subjects lacks depth. There
is no pattern or progression in the subjects that are
covered. Workshops do not build in any purposeful or
continuing way on those that have come before. The
American Library Association has the responsibility of
improving continuing education.

175. "Rules for Public Librarian Certification and Public Li-

brary System Certification." _Wisconsin Library_

Bulletin. 68 (July-August 1972), 199-202.

Presented is the text of the _Wisconsin Administrative_
Code section for the Department of Public Instruction as
pertains to public librarian and public library system
certification. No specific requirement for continuing
education is stipulated for public librarian certification. However, each library system is required to have
an in-service training program for library personnel
within the system by the end of its third year of operatic

176. Schiller, Anita R. Characteristics of Professional Per-

sonnel in College and University Libraries. Urbana:

University of Illinois Graduate School of Library

Science, Library Research Center, 1968. 118p.

The objectives of this survey were to describe the
characteristics of librarians employed on the staffs of
the more than 2,000 higher educational institutions in
the United States in 1966-67, and to identify and examine
relevant manpower issues. The report is based on the
responses of 2,282 individuals, or 93 percent of 2,459
sampled full-time employees. Geographic origin, age,
marital and family status, professional and academic
degrees held, present positions, academic status and rank,
and salaries are reported for all academic librarians,
and for men and women. Data from other relevant studies
are used to indicate trends and comparisons. Major, manpower issues are seen as--the importance of challenging
work as a characteristic of the library career, recognition
of special problems in librarianship where women are a
numerical majority, need to eliminate discrimination
importance of full faculty status for academic librarians,
and the need for more equitable salaries.

177. Schwartz, Mortimer. "Paraprofessionals and Law Librarian-

ship: A Preliminary Perspective." Law Library

Journal. 66 (February 1973), 3-11.

A paraprofessional who works in a library of any kind
is referred to as a library technician or as a library
technical assistant. The law library paraprofessional
does a mixture of high level clerical tasks and low level
professional routines. The legal profession has been
exploring how paraprofessionals might be employed
effectively in law practice. Professional meetings at
the local, state, and national levels have discussed the

topic. Training institutes which are privately operated
and profit-seeking have sprung up to train paraprofessiona
for the legal profession. This article explores the concept of paraprofessionalism within the framework of law
librarianship. There is a general discussion of the role
of the paraprofessional and a broad outline of a possible
training program for paraprofessionals in law library work
and related areas such as government documents and social
science library service.

178. Shank, Russell. "Administration Training in Graduate

Library Schools." Special Libraries. 58 (January

1967), 30-32.

Special library administration is not offered as a
separate course in eleven U.S. accredited library schools.
Instead, a general course covers the principles of administration for all types of libraries. Library School
faculty feel that too much information would be repeated
if courses in administration were taught for public,
school, academic, and special libraries. Faculty prefer
to deal with each of these types of libraries within the
framework of general library administration.

179. Shera, Jesse H. "Self-destructing Diploma." Ohio Library

Association Bulletin. 42 (October 1972), 4-8.

The author gives a brief history of continuing professional library education with special emphasis on Ohio.
History indicates that the awareness of the need for
continuing education rises during periods of rapid change
and professional stress--when the old order is threatened.
Recommendations are offered for making continuing education programs a success. Learning should be cumulative,
based on information learned in earlier sessions. Participants must be actively involved in learning. Reports,
exercises, even tests or examinations should lead the

student toward a goal. Various types of libraries and
state agencies should cooperate with adequate financing
arranged.

180. Shubert, Joseph F. A Community Librarian's Training Pro-

gram. A Report on a New Mexico Program and Guide-

lines for Developing Training Programs Based Upon

Correspondence Study and Adult Education Techniques.

Boulder, Colorado: Western Interstate Commission

for Higher Education, 1973. 34p.

The Western Interstate Commission on Higher Education
(WICHE) developed a continuing education program for
public library assistants. The New Mexico State Library
and WICHE cooperated in the testing and evaluation of
the correspondence course. This manual demonstrates how
this method can be replicated by library agencies in
other states or regional systems. The Community Library
Training Program is geared towards staff in public libraries and institutions who cannot attend university
courses because of time, money, or distance. Correspondence work and study sessions provide a basic library background. Discussion of the value of practical experience
in a work situation over a considerable period of time
is included.

181. Shubert, Joseph F. "Continuing Education in Ohio."

Illinois Libraries. 56 (June 1974), 471-76.

Mr. Shubert, the State Librarian, suggests that a
commitment of financial resources for insuring a high
quality statewide program of continuing education and
staff development might be as high as 1 percent of the
total expenditures by all libraries in the state of Ohio.
By this standard, no less than $1.2 million should be
directed at meeting the continuing education needs of all
types of library personnel throughout the state.

As a means of putting together information on selected continuing education programs in FY 1973, data were assembled on workshops which were assisted directly or indirectly by LSCA funds, or in which State Library personnel carried some specific responsibility. The data are summarized.

Recent discussion with the State Library Board's Advisory Council on Federal Library Programs drew the following conclusions that the responsibility for continuing efficient and effective personnel is shared as follows: 1) individual responsibility must be assumed for the reading of current literature and for structuring a personal program which will permit attendance at certain professional conferences, institutes, and workshops; 2) individual libraries should sponsor in-service training at the various levels of staff competence to insure maximum library service; 3) the various associations whose membership concerns focus on library and information specialties can provide a source of exceptional expertise from which to develop continuing education programs; 4) library schools have a continuing obligation to assist in the continuing education of alumni and other librarians alike; and 5) the important staff and financial resources of the State Library provide an important foundation for the development of a coordinated and cooperative program of continuing education and staff development among all concerned groups.

182. Simmons, B. S. "Professional Development." Catholic

Library World. 43 (October 1971), 79-82.

Since the period of formal training for librarians is brief, it is imperative that they be continually developing. Although no agency is assuming responsibility for planning, the individual librarian should be responsible for his own professional growth.

183. Simpson, Anthony E. "Graduate Study Benefits for the Li-

brary Employee in Manhattan." <u>Journal of Education</u>

<u>for Librarianship</u>. 12 (Summer 1971), 40-47.

Prior to the fall of 1970, the New York Public Library made funds available for its professional employees
to obtain a second master's or other advanced degrees.
Since that time, however, the scholarship fund is limited
to library school students working in the research libraries. To study the situation further, the author made
a comparison of the tuition benefits granted to librarians
employed throughout the city to ascertain whether the
policies of the public library systems were a fair reflection of those practiced by other employing institutions. The responses of forty academic and special libraries are analyzed concerning tuition benefits. Two
conclusions are: 1) regardless of the size of the library, almost half of those surveyed offer substantial
financial aid toward the tuition costs of employees seeking advanced degrees through part-time study; and
2) 39 percent of the libraries permit their professional
employees to attend classes on library time.

184. Slavens, Thomas P. and Legg, Jean M. "Experimenting in

Education for Library Associates." <u>Journal of Edu-</u>

<u>cation for Librarianship</u>. 11 (Fall 1970), 182-85.

There are many capable and educated people who are
on library staffs but do not have a degree from a library
school and do not have the time to attend such a school
because of time, money, or distance. The authors make
some general observations about ways of providing education for these people so they can do more than clerical
work and serve beside professional librarians as library
associates. Careful planning is recommended. A library
can work through state libraries, library school faculties,
extension departments of universities, and in state
departments of education. Planning for such programs
includes specifying instructional objectives, determining
whether examinations will be given, organizing reading

lists, soliciting guest lecturers, approximating cost,
and specifying length of the program. In order for the
courses to be successful, participants must return to
their libraries with positions of greater responsibility.

185. Sloane, Margaret N. Continuing Education for Special Li-

brarianship; Where Do We Go from Here? New York:

1968. 62p. ED 032 086.

During the three-hour planning session 125 representatives from twenty Special Libraries Association
chapters discussed the need for continuing education
for special librarians, the structure and the content of
continuing education.

186. Sloane, Margaret N. "Special Library Association Chapters

and Continuing Education." Special Libraries. 58

(January 1967), 24-26.

The primary responsibility for continuing education
should be with the SLA chapters. This can be accomplished
through workshops and seminars co-sponsored, if desirable,
with the local library schools in the area. The Chapters
are more flexible and are not constrained by funding and
allocations as are government agencies, academic institutions, SLA Headquarters, and others. The practical workshop concerned with current problems is extremely benefici

187. Sollenberger, Judith K. In-Service Training; A Biblio-

graphical Essay. rev. ed. American Library Associa-

tion, 1965. 25p.

This bibliography covers in-service training in libraries, 1955-1964; it includes programs conducted within
individual libraries and those organized outside the library to a greater or lesser degree. The bibliography

includes a selection of titles concerning personnel,
management, and efficiency outside the field of libraries.
In-service training is divided into the following categories: professional training, preprofessional training,
internships, training in special areas of library service,
training in small and rural libraries, and evaluation.

188. Special Libraries Association. "Continuing Education for

Special Librarianship . . . Where Do We Go from Here?"

Proceedings of a Planning Session Sponsored by the

Education Committee, held June 2, 1968 in Conjunction

with the Special Libraries Association. Annual

Conference in Los Angeles. (Mimeographed)

189. "Standing Committee on Continuing Library Education."

Journal of Education for Librarianship. 13 (Fall

1972), 137-43.

The American Association of Library Schools adopted
a position paper on continuing library education at its
1972 annual meeting. This article lists the liaison
representatives from the accredited graduate library
schools.

A summary of discussions and action of the Standing
Committee on Continuing Library Education is also given.

190. Stevenson, Grace T. "Training for Growth--the Future for

Librarians." ALA Bulletin. 61 (March 1967), 278-86.

Emphasized is the need for continuing education
beyond the MLS degree. Some of this training will be on
the university campus but extension courses, workshops,

and institutes are also necessary. ALA, state library
associations, and state libraries should all take some
responsibility in this area.

191. Stone, Elizabeth W. "Administrators Fiddle While
       Employees Burn or Flee." <u>ALA Bulletin</u>. 63
       (February 1969), 181-87.

     The consensus of those librarians responding to a
questionnaire on the effectiveness of library administrators indicates that administrators are trying to conduct library business with outdated methods. Recommended is an asset management approach which is concerned
with the best allocation of resources. Four ways of
motivating librarians toward self-development are also
suggested.

192. Stone, Elizabeth W. "Continuing Education: Avenue to
       Adventure." <u>School Libraries</u>. 18 (Summer 1969),
       37-46.

     Formally or informally, a school librarian must
expect to continue his education for the duration of his
professional life. The "adventurous" librarian realizes
that his formal education is merely a stepping-stone,
is a self-starter, has a disposition to innovation and
experimentation, is willing to have his performance
measured and evaluated. All these factors are dependent
on continuing professional education.

193. Stone, Elizabeth W. "Continuing Education in Librarian-

       ship; Ideas for Action." <u>American Libraries</u>. 1

       (June 1970), 543-51.

     A survey on continuing education for librarians
brought 879 suggestions for action. Specific and general
recommendations are made to administrators, to library
associations, to library schools, to planners in the U.S.

Office of Education, to statewide library planners, and
to the individual librarian. The breadth of these recommendations illustrates clearly that the librarians sampled
hold all of these relevant groups accountable for providing favorable conditions for their professional development. In their opinion, continuing education is a nationwide problem for which a cooperative nationwide plan
based on the best thinking and planning of a national
assembly of all relevant groups is the best solution.

194. Stone, Elizabeth W. <u>Continuing Library Education as
     Viewed in Relation to Other Continuing Professional
     Education Movements</u>. Washington, D.C.: American
     Society for Information Science, 1974 (in press).

195. Stone, Elizabeth W. <u>Factors Related to the Professional
     Development of Librarians</u>. Metuchen, New Jersey:
     The Scarecrow Press, 1969. 281p.

This study was undertaken to determine some of the
factors that motivate librarians to continue their professional development after receiving the master's degree
in library science. Conversely, it also sought to
identify some of the factors which might deter professional development activities. The findings showed a
significant disparity between what the librarians were
doing and what they thought they should be doing for
maximum professional development. The entire sample preferred activities that were somewhat informal and which
provided social contacts with other professionals.

The 879 respondents had several suggestions for
continuing professional growth. Library administrators
received the most advice. They should allow librarians
to have paid sabbaticals for study or research. Administrators should arrange to pay for professional

activities. Pay raises should be determined by professional growth. Administrators were also advised to find
out what is going on in their own libraries and to improve themselves in administration skills and in adapting
to change.

196. Stone, Elizabeth W. <u>Highlights from the Final Report of</u>

<u>the Continuing Library and Information Science Edu-</u>

<u>cation Project</u>. National Commission on Libraries

and Information Science, Washington, D.C.: U.S.

Government Printing Office, 1974. 8p.

(See entry no. 202 for annotation.)

197. Stone, Elizabeth W. "Librarians and Continuing Education."

<u>Journal of Education for Librarianship</u>. 11 (Summer

1970), 64-71.

A questionnaire was distributed to a random group of
librarians assessing their motivation to participate in
continuing education programs. Both encouraging and
deterring factors are listed. Inability to meet the
criteria of accessibility, convenience in timing, and
support from supervisors will tend to keep the librarian
from participating in the continuing education opportunity.
Positive factors are: content of the program is related
to the work process or to the jobs the librarian is doing;
the opportunities for professional development need to
be set forth and described so that librarians can ascertain if the activities are geared to meet their individual
needs; and long-range goals must be stated more clearly
and should be implemented through joint planning by
groups sharing responsibility in the area of continuing
education.

198. Stone, Elizabeth W., ed. <u>New Directions in Staff Develop-</u>

<u>ment; Moving from Ideas to Action</u>. The Papers of a

One-Day Conference Held in Detroit, Michigan,

June 28, 1970. Sponsored by the Staff Development

Committee, ALA. Chicago: American Library Associa-

tion, 1971. 66p.

  The papers presented in this one-day conference
stress three points: 1) continuing personnel development
is an important commitment librarianship must face; 2) librarianship is a long way from realizing the potential
represented by the human resources now employed in libraries; and 3) the American Library Association has a
role in personnel development and should emphatically
foster continuing education of its membership. Topics
include, "Planning for a Statewide Continuing Professional
Education Program," "Participative Management in Libraries," and "Incentives and Motivation for Staff Development."

199. Stone, Elizabeth W. "Quest for Expertise: A Librarian's

Responsibility." <u>College and Research Libraries</u>.

32 (November 1971), 432-441.

  This article focuses attention on librarians to see
what gaps exist between perceived importance and actual
involvement in the area of the academic librarian's professional development and to develop action planning on
the basis of the data. Two signs of a professional are
the individual's desire to continually seek opportunities for development and further learning, and his
realization that the main instrument or "tool" for him as
a professional is himself and how creatively he can use
his talents and training.

200. Stone, Elizabeth W. "Role of AALS in Lifetime Learning

for Librarians." Journal of Education for Librarian-

ship. 12 (Spring 1972), 254-66.

The Study Committee on Continuing Education of the
American Association of Library Schools saw its primary
mission as delineating the role of AALS in continuing
library education. The committee felt the need for
concerted effort and coordination of all relevant groups,
and attached to its report an appendix dealing with
goals, criteria, and components relative to national
planning for continuing library education. Library
schools should begin work with professions outside of
librarianship; AALS should develop the resources so that
practicing librarians can take any needed course in any
geographic area at any time.

201. Stone, Elizabeth W. "Summary of Responses to Data Sheet

on Continuing Education as it Exists in Library

Associations from Six Responding Library Associa-

tions: 1972." Available from the Illini Union

Bookstore, University of Illinois, Champaign,

Illinois.

The summary consists of ninety-six categories covering a variety of topics on use of cable TV, a listing of
the continuing educational objectives of the library
associations, institutes or seminars offered or developed.

202. Stone, Elizabeth W. Training for the Improvement of Li-

brary Administration. Champaign: University of

Illinois, Graduate School of Library Science, 1967.

83p.

Half of the graduates from library schools who stay
in library work for five years or more have administrative
responsibility to direct the work of others whether it be
in a department, a branch, a school library, or as a
head librarian. However, one of the greatest weaknesses
in librarianship is its lack of training in administrative and supervisory skills. The quality of library
service is in part determined by the middle management
and supervisory skills of those librarians. This study
gives a general picture of training in library administration. Topics covered are: a review of the developing
concepts of library administration over the last eighty
years; the contribution of library schools in teaching
library administration; an analysis of the process of
management; and others.

203. Stone, Elizabeth W. and Patrick, Ruth J. <u>Continuing Li-</u>

   <u>brary Education Center: A Design for Action</u>. The

   Catholic University of America, 1974. 40p.

   This report is a preliminary draft of the recommendations from the Continuing Library and Information Science
Education Project sponsored by the National Commission
on Libraries and Information Science. A model for continuing library education is outlined for consideration
by participating members. This document presents a
nationwide plan for the continuing education of library
personnel.

204. Stone, Elizabeth W., Patrick, Ruth J., and Conroy, Barbara.

   <u>Continuing Library and Information Science Education</u>.

   <u>Final Report</u>. National Commission on Libraries and

   Information Science. Washington, D.C.: U.S.

   Government Printing Office, 1974. various paging.

This report and its recommendations are based on a nine-month study of a proposed nationwide program of continuing education for personnel in the library and information science field. Some of the major issues studied are: certification, organizational and individual incentives for continuing education, educational methods, and continuing education needs. One major recommendation proposed is a Continuing Library Education Network and Exchange (CLENE) which is intended to provide easy access to leadership expertise, and program and resource assistance. It would provide a facility designed to meet individual needs and to develop and strengthen leadership within the library profession at all levels.

A critique of three alternative models for a national plan for continuing library education is also given. An extensive bibliography includes monographs, articles, and reports on continuing education not only in library and information science but also in other professions.

205. Sullivan, Peggy A., ed. "Staff Development: A Continuing

Theme with Variations." School Media Quarterly. 1

(Spring 1973), 179-200.

A series of four articles discusses the need for continuing education of school librarians. Focus is placed on the need for continual development of the professional librarian through pre-service curriculum and postgraduate work; a description of the MILE (Multimedia Individualized Learning Experience) in-service program at the Dubuque, Iowa community schools; the short-term institute as a vehicle for continuing education; and the use of instructional media in in-service education of teachers.

206. "System Development Corporation to Design a Series of On-

the-Job Training Courses." Bookmark. 27 (December

1967), 141.

The U.S. Office of Education has funded a $185,000 project in which the System Development Corporation will design a series of in-service training courses for professionals and nonprofessionals in all types of libraries throughout the U.S. The project has two phases. First, investigators will analyze operational requirements of libraries not being met because of lack of knowledge or skills among the library staff. Researchers will determine what new skills are needed for staff to learn a systems approach to library operations and work with automation specialists. Instruction techniques and tools will then be developed. Phase II will consist of training courses being tested at selected libraries throughout the country. The courses will be applicable for professional librarians, library clerks, subject specialists, technicians, and systems specialists.

207. Tyer, Travis E., ed. "Continuing Education." *Illinois Libraries*. 56 (June 1974),432-500. ED 093 361.

The above issue of *Illinois Libraries* is devoted to current practices in the continuing education of library personnel in the midwestern United States with some emphasis on the role of library associations and state libraries. Allan B. Knox, Director of the Office of Continuing Education and Public Services, University of Illinois at Urbana-Champaign, discusses the theoretical and philosophical aspects of continuing education for librarianship. Allie Beth Martin offers a model for a coordinated program for all library personnel involving all relevant organizations and agencies. An article on Lincoln Open University in Illinois concerns individualized instruction outside the formal academic setting. Other articles focus on current activities in Illinois, Missouri, Ohio, Michigan, and Wisconsin.

208. Tyer, Travis E. "Continuing Education for Librarianship in Illinois." *Illinois Libraries*. 56 (June 1974), 442-54.

Illinois has played an active role in fostering continuing education for librarians. Mr. Tyer, a State Library Consultant, summarizes the results of a study of education and training activities in Illinois, 1966-1970. Education and training activities conducted by the Library Systems varied widely in subject, frequency, and attendance. The author provides additional candid information on the successes and failures of activities of the Systems, 1970 to date. During this time Systems have emphasized trustee education and reference service. The activities of the Illinois Library Association, the Illinois Chapter of the Special Library Association, and the State Library are also detailed.

Three recommendations are offered: 1) less emphasis is needed on the type of library in which the target audience is employed while greater emphasis should be placed on the needs of the library community at large; 2) all levels of library employees (both professionals and nonprofessionals) of all types of libraries must have the opportunity for continuing education; and 3) all relevant agencies and groups must find a means of building incentive within each individual trustee and library staff member to participate and profit from those activities.

209. United States Civil Service Commission. <u>Library Planning,</u>

<u>Organizing, and Evaluating Training Programs</u>.

Personnel Bibliography Series, no. 18. Washington, D.C

The Library, 1966.

210. Vainstein, Rose. "What the Library Schools Can Do in the

    Training and Upgrading of Consultants." In

    Guy Garrison, ed. The Changing Role of State Library

    Consultants. Champaign, Illinois: The University

    of Illinois, Graduate School of Library Science,

    1968. pp. 83-95.

Trained state library consultants can strengthen and effect a statewide program of library excellence. The initial and continuous education of such consultants must be carefully planned. Consultants are in a unique position to assist and coordinate library service to all types of libraries. That they have not done so may be because training programs have not been available. Library schools are deficient in offering formal course work in consultant education. In-service training of consultants on an ongoing basis is minimal at best. The author recommends post-master's training for consultants through internship programs. State libraries and library schools need to work closely together in this effort.

211. Verschoor, Irving A. "Planning for Personnel." In:

    Herbert A. Carl, ed. Statewide Long-Range Planning

    for Libraries. Washington, D.C.: U.S. Department

    of Health, Education and Welfare, 1966. pp. 35-42.

Library personnel function in a broad organizational structure which is continually undergoing change. Librarians interact as members of a social group. In the area of personnel training, the author recommends: 1) the establishment of a post-master's degree program in some of the library schools; 2) greater effort to utilize available personnel resources; 3) more stress on

training programs for supporting personnel; 4) more attention given to pre-professional trainee programs; 5) dual
certification for the teacher as a librarian; and 6) the
formalization of training of clerical personnel. To
carry out such programs requires thoughtful planning.
The author offers a few ideas for effecting an overall
plan for personnel development.

212. Verschoor, Irving A. Tasks and Training of Personnel in

Community Libraries in New York State, 1958-1966.

222p.

213. Walker, Richard D. "Independent Study Materials in Li-

brary Science Instruction." Journal of Education

for Librarianship. 10 (Summer 1969), 44-52.

Programmed learning materials called AIM were
developed at the Extension Division of the University of
Wisconsin. They were used in independent study courses
offered off-campus for full academic credit. The author
developed an experimental design to compare the effectiveness of the programmed materials with that of class instruction. The conclusions are that there is no differ-
ence in the level of retention between students who receive
catalog instruction by the conventional lecture-laboratory
method and those who receive catalog instruction in an
independent programmed format. It can be concluded that
independent study materials are useful learning techniques
and can be utilized for students who cannot attend classes
in a formal university setting.

214. Wallace, Everett M. and Katter, Robert V. Research and

Development of On-the-Job Training Courses for

Library Personnel. Final Report. Santa Monica,

California: System Development Corp., 1969. 84p.

ED 032 085.

The purpose of this project was to research and develop instructional materials for use in on-the-job training of professional and nonprofessional library staff in technical and scientific libraries. One instructional package is directed toward professional librarians and provides an introduction to systems analysis. The initial project covers: 1) reference tools and procedures, 2) foreign and technical terminology, and 3) applications of modern technology in libraries. The training approach emphasizes flexibility and modularity in the course materials and trainee-directed self-testing and study. The authors also list previous research, design, and development activities.

215. Warncke, Ruth E. "Continuing Education: Whose Responsibility?" Minnesota Libraries. 24 (Autumn 1973), 59-65.

Continuing professional education is the "acquisition of specialized knowledge designed to enable one to function more effectively in achieving the goals of his job and of the institution in which he works." Types of learning opportunities are discussed. Library literature is a valuable resource for the individual to keep abreast of the profession but there is too much duplication of information in the journals and not enough specialization. Library meetings, institutes, and workshops are also valuable resources for continuing education but must be well planned and thought-out for maximum learning to take place. The state library association should shoulder the responsibility for continuing education because it is the only library entity that involves people from every type of institution and service. Through its members, it has access to all kinds of specialized knowledge. The state association can coordinate continuing education programs that build upon strength. It can develop cooperation with other states, supply publicity, and sponsor scholarships.

216. Webster, Duane E. "The Management Review and Analysis

Program: An Assisted Self-Study to Secure Con-

structive Change in the Management of Research Li-

braries." College and Research Libraries. 35

(March 1974), 114-25.

The Association of Research Libraries, Office of
University Library Management Studies, designed, tested,
and operated the Management Review and Analysis Program
(MRAP). Large academic and research libraries can use
the assisted self-study strategy in reviewing and
analyzing their on-going management policies and procedures. MRAP offers guidelines for the implementation
of current principles of management for the improvement
of library programs.

217. Webster, Duane E. Plan for Development of the Office of

University Management Studies. Washington, D.C.:

Council on Library Resources, 9p. ED 063 002.

This is a summary of a report submitted by the
management consulting firm of Booz, Allen and Hamilton,
Inc. It concerns a study of the staffing and organization of the Columbia University Libraries for the Association of Research Libraries (ARL). Presented is a plan
for the conduct of management programs that contribute
to the ARL's goal of strengthening the services and
collections of member libraries. The purpose of the
Management Studies Office is to assist university research libraries in serving their users through sound
management of available resources. The Office focuses on
budget, supervision, management, planning policies, staff
development, personnel, management information, and organization. Four projects are to be handled by the
Office concerning library management: 1) a research and
development program, 2) publication program, 3) conference
program, and 4) consultation. The Management Studies
Office is a part of ARL.

218. White, Rodney F. and Macklin, David B. Education Careers

and Professionalization in Librarianship and In-

formation Science. Final Report. College Park,

Maryland: School of Library and Information Services,

University of Maryland, 1970. 180p. ED 054 800.

This study analyzes the processes by which individuals choose the occupation of librarianship and are
prepared for professional positions. Educational institutions are studied in terms of their training of
students. ALA accredited library schools in the U.S. and
Canada are included in the mail surveys of students and
faculty. Results of on-site visits to a majority of the
schools are also given. Discussions and interviews were
conducted with both faculty and students during site
visits. Both groups wanted improvements in existing library school programs, especially technological changes
rather than intellectual aspects. Although faculty see
the need for reform, the prospects for reform are dim and,
as a result, library school curricula will encounter increasing competition from other departments of the university.

219. Wildman, Iris J. "Education: A Lifelong Process." Law

Library Journal. 65 (May 1972), 130-33.

This article concerns the need for law librarians to
keep up with an ever-changing subject field. The role of
the institute as a tool of continuing education in this
area is discussed, as well as the necessity of the librarian's continued awareness of changes in classification, subject control, and reference tools.

220. Wilson, Patrick. "Library Schooling and the Education of

Professionals." California Librarian. 33

(October 1972), 194-98.

The author is Dean of the School of Librarianship at the University of California-Berkeley. He advocates the axiom that what precedes and what follows library school-ing is more important in molding a good professional than what occurs in the year or two of formal library education.

There are two philosophies concerning the role of li-brary school education--the minimalist and maximalist views. The former view aims at furnishing the student with an adequate inventory of detailed, specific in-struction; the latter view attempts to give the student a general grasp of the librarian's situation so he can become a good general problem solver. The author favors the maximalist view because librarianship is complex and library schools cannot provide all the answers to all situations. If the librarian thinks that continuing edu-cation is an optional luxury, then that person is not a professional. If everything could be learned in one year then librarianship would not be a profession.

221. Younger, Jane. "Continuing Education and LSCA: the

Division [for Library Services] Helps Librarians

Improve Skills." Wisconsin Library Bulletin. 69

(July 1973), 224-26.

This article chronicles the role of Wisconsin's Division for Library Services in continuing professional education since 1959. With the help of LSCA funds, the Division has offered a program of scholarships to stu-dents of library science, cooperates and coordinates continuing education programs with other educational agencies and institutions; and sponsors workshops and publications to keep library personnel and board members informed on new developments. The Division has helped develop the Educational Telephone Network (ETN) to pre-sent library science courses to update personnel. Several other programs in cable TV and game simulation are also detailed.

222. Younger, Jane. "The Continuing Education Scene in

      Wisconsin." <u>Illinois Libraries</u>. 56 (June 1974),

      476-79.

    In its long-range plan, Wisconsin has included as
one of its goals to determine the continuing education
needs of library personnel. The plan further urges that
the Educational Telephone Network for librarian education
be continued. Through use of open-air telephone lines a
giant "party line" is set up which allows all participants to hear and be heard. The network has outlets
located in county courthouses, University of Wisconsin
campuses, libraries, and hospitals in more than one
hundred Wisconsin communities. Some of the programs
offered over the network are described.

    Wisconsin is awaiting the conclusion of the study of
continuing educational needs by the Council on Library
Development's Manpower Task Force. The state will make
goals and objectives based on the findings of the study.

223. Youngs, W. O. "Continuing Education for Librarianship."

      <u>PNLA Quarterly</u>. 29 (January 1965), 122-26.

    Since library school education prepares the young
professional primarily for work on the beginning level,
further training is needed to improve his abilities as
subject specialist, cataloger, documents librarian, or
whatever. Emphasized is on-the-job training and several
examples are cited.

224. Zachert, Martha Jane K. "Continuing Education for Li-

      brarians: The Role of the Learner." In:

      Eleanor E. Goehring, ed. University of Tennessee

      Library Lectures Numbers Twenty-two, Twenty-three,

      and Twenty-four. 1970-72. Knoxville, Tennessee:

      The University of Tennessee, 1972. p. 30-52.

There has been no overall planning for continuing education because there has been so little systematic planning for basic professional education. The research by psychologists and curriculum planners on curriculum development has not been utilized in planning library science education. Adult learning research shows that adults learn differently than children. There is a strong relationship between motivation and participation in continuing education. For adults, it is interaction that produces learning--interaction in relation to problem-solving, learner-identified problems, and individual experience. The author summarizes some of the findings of recent research about adult learning and briefly explores their implications for continuing education.

B. In-Service Training

225. "Action Alternatives." American Libraries. 5 (February

1974), 67.

Librarians at the Riverside (California) City and
County Public Library are participating in a course,
"Action Alternatives for Community Change," offered by
the Extension Division of the University of California,
Riverside. Participants learn the techniques of working
toward governmental, social, or educational change they
wish to effect. Members learn how to organize for change,
surmount obstacles, evaluate progress, and change direction
when necessary.

So far three teams from the library have taken the
class which meets two days a month for four months.
Each team must choose a feasible project that can be
operational before the program ends. One project is
related to library publicity.

226. Adams, Kathryn. "Regional In-service Training Projects

in Louisiana During 1968-69." Louisiana Library

Association Bulletin. 32 (Winter 1970), 167-69.

This article gives a description of the emphasis and
content of four regional in-service training programs
designed to assist public libraries in improving service
through better-trained nonprofessional and professional
staff.

227. American Library Association. Library Education Division.

Continuing Educations for Librarians 1971. Chicago:

American Library Association, 1971.

This directory lists formal programs of continuing
library education in the United States. Not included are

the institutes in various areas of librarianship supported by the Office of Education under the Higher Education Act.

Among formal programs, school librarianship received the heaviest emphasis. Second were programs on
services to children and young people. Library automation
was third.

The continuing education programs available to librarians in 1970 were overwhelmingly sponsored by
accredited library schools (39) and other institutions
of higher education (39).

228. American Library Association. Library Education Division.

"Continuing Education for Librarians: Conferences,

Workshops, and Short Courses, 1968." ALA Library

Education Division Newsletter. 67 (November 1968),

23-33.

229. American Library Association. Library Education Division.

Continuing Education for Librarians: Conferences,

Workshops, and Short Courses, 1969-1970. Chicago:

American Library Association, 1969.

230. American Library Association. Library Education Division.

"Continuing Education for Librarians: Conferences,

Workshops, and Short Courses, 1970." ALA Library Edu

cation Division Newsletter. 72 (March 1970), 14-26;

73 (April 1970), 7-9; 74 (September 1970), 13-14.

231. American Library Association. Library Education Division. "Continuing Education for Librarians: Conferences, Workshops, and Short Courses, 1971." ALA Library Education Division Newsletter. 75 (December 1970), 13-19; 76 (March 1971), 13-18; 77 (June 1971), 15-19.

232. American Library Association. Library Education Division. "Continuing Education for Librarians: Conferences, Workshops, Short Courses, 1972." American Libraries. 2 (December 1971), 1217-19.

First Supplement, 3 (February 1972), 179-81.

Second Supplement, 3 (April 1972), 423-26.

Third Supplement, 3 (June 1972), 662-64.

233. Bracken, M. C. and Shilling, C. W. Survey of Practical Training in Information Science. George Washington University, 1968. 28p.

Summary. American Documentation. 19 (April 1968), 113-19.

This paper presents a survey of practical training being conducted in the United States. All the universities known by the authors to have programs to train information scientists and all the industrial organizations known or thought to have programs for this type of training are surveyed. No qualitative assessments are made by the authors. Rather, quantitative results of the survey are presented on various program characteristics.

234. Cashman, Mary E. and Cox, William H. "Recruitment in One

Public Library." ALA Bulletin. 59 (Fall 1965),

147-50.

In the 1950's and 1960's recruitment to the library
profession was a problem. Since two influential factors
in the selection of librarianship as a career are contact
with a librarian and work experience in a library, a
recruitment program was carried on within the library.
The Rochester Public Library in New York set up a libraria
trainee program. Students were placed in pre-professional
positions in which they would learn library skills while
performing professional duties under guidance. Trainees
were encouraged to attain a master's degree in library
science within four years. Afterward, they were expected
to seek employment with the Rochester Public Library for
at least two years.

235. Conroy, Barbara. A Descriptive and Evaluative Report of

the Washington Seminar Library Career Development

Institute. Washington, D.C.: Department of Library

Science, The Catholic University·of America, 1971.

115p.

The basic objective of the above Institute was "to
enable individuals to develop their leadership potential
and their ability to evidence that leadership in the
field of librarianship" at the managerial level. This
report describes the learning model used in the Institute
and its suitability for continuing education efforts
sponsored by library schools, staff development programs,
and professional associations. The description of the
model includes aspects of organization and administration, recruitment and selection of participants. The
evaluation of the model includes its major strengths
and weaknesses, and both actual and anticipated outcomes.
Appendices list the materials used in the Institute.

236. "Continuing Education Plan Reports Success in New York."

Library Journal. 94 (January 15, 1969), 135-36.

The Westchester Library Association and the New York University School of Continuing Education cooperated on a program of continuing education for librarians. Results after one year of operation are briefly summarized. Reactions to the course were favorable. Some participants have since been given more responsibility or have received a pay increase.

237. "Continuing Education for Pros and Non-pros." Library

Journal. 99 (October 15, 1974), 2570.

Two items on continuing education are listed. The first concerns a three-day continuing education seminar on handling exhibition catalogs. The National Commission on Libraries and Information Science is sponsoring the programs statewide for both professional and nonprofessional personnel.

The second item deals with a correspondence/seminar course. The New Mexico State Library has awarded a $10,000 grant to the College of the Southwest for a Community Librarians Training Program consisting of a correspondence course plus a series of seminars. A total of thirty students across the state will take Loyola University's correspondence course--Public Library Service--and exchange ideas in seminars slated for different areas of the state.

238. "Converting Bachelors to Masters." Wilson Library

Bulletin. 48 (January 1974), 362.

"At Louisiana State University, graduates with a B.S. in library service can turn it into a master's by completing twelve hours of additional work and passing a written comprehensive final examination. The new program began in Spring, 1974 in Baton Rouge."

239. Davis, E. H. "Fiji and Beyond: East-West Center's

    Refresher Course for Library Assistants." Hawaii

    Library Association Journal. 26 (June 1969), 14-22.

       A unique experiment in international library educa-
tion for library assistants has been going on in the
South Pacific and Asia since 1966. The East-West Center,
located in Hawaii, offers a program titled, "Refresher
Course for Library Assistants." Since a course participant is often the only person in charge of a library,
training is given in all areas of library science.
Described are the subjects taught in the program, the
background of the participants, and the criteria for thei.
selection into the program. The East-West Center provide
transportation for the students, a daily stipend, in-
surance, and books. Students pay no tuition. The progra
is approximately five months in length with twelve to
seventeen students participating per class. Theory and
practical experience are combined in various types of
libraries in Hawaii.

240. Davis, Kay. "Continuing Education in Missouri." Illinoi

    Libraries. 56 (June 1974), 462-65.

       Continuing education for librarians in Missouri bega
on a statewide basis in the late 1950's. With enabling
funds from the Library Services Act of 1956, development
has been continuous and growing. The State Library and
the University of Missouri library school have been the
primary sources in setting up workshops for library
staff at all levels. The Missouri Association of School
Librarians hold two statewide meetings a year with
emphasis on "how to."

       The Grand River Library Conference consists of the
public libraries in twelve northern counties. It meets
on a quarterly basis featuring topics of current interest
to librarians. Dates and locations of workshops and institutes for trustees, librarians, and nonprofessionals
are included at the end of the article.

241.   Davis, Marie A.   "In-service Training for Adult Service

Librarians."   Adult Services Division Newsletter.

(Spring 1966), 4-6.

Since 1953, the Free Library of Philadelphia has
sponsored in-service training on a systematic basis for
its staff.   The library's objectives are to broaden professional outlook, underline techniques learned in library school, reinforce the service concept, adapt the
staff's library education and experience to the Free
Library's basic goals, and have staff learn of the library's role in the Philadelphia and Pennsylvania
communities.

The organization of the workshops is described.   An
outline of the 1965-66 sessions is given.   Workshops
usually cover book selection policy and librarians' review,
readers services, and programming techniques.

242.   "Education in Orbit."   Wilson Library Bulletin.   49

(September 1974), 11-12.

This is an announcement of a satellite program to
educate librarians in outlying areas of a dozen mountain
and plains states.   The University of Denver Graduate
School of Librarianship, under a $117,000 HEW grant, will
provide a year's funding to plan programs that will train
in-service librarians at the professional and the paraprofessional levels via programs beamed to the educational
satellite which will be launched in December 1975.

This training activity will be part of a broad range
of library-related programming for a two-year period.

243.   Franckowiak, Bernard.   "ETN for In-service Growth."

Wisconsin Library Bulletin.   65 (March 1969), 86.

An experimental series of in-service workshops for
librarians and audiovisual personnel was held using the
Education Telephone Network (ETN).   Participants in 31

cities in Wisconsin were shown a slide presentation and received handouts of materials. The phone lines allowed participants to ask questions.

Addresses are given so anyone can write to borrow the audiovisual materials or a copy of the tapes.

244. Fry, R. M. "Commitment to Change." _Missouri Library_

Association Quarterly. 30 (March 1969), 58-64.

Following the premise that "there is nothing permanent except change," the author discusses some of the federal programs of the mid-1960s that offered institutes and training programs for librarians.

245. Fuller, Muriel L. "What One Library School Has Done:

A Case Study." In: Guy Garrison, ed. _The_

Changing Role of State Library Consultants.

Champaign, Illinois: The University of Illinois

Graduate School of Library Science, 1968, pp. 75-82.

The University of Wisconsin Library School has a sixth-year specialist program which offers training opportunities for library consultants. A course is given in public library systems; institutes and workshops are geared to consultants' problems. State Library staff are resource specialists who serve as guest speakers and course lecturers. The Director of the Division for Library Services and his field services staff cooperatively plan the on-going training programs. Each course in the program is described. Details of some of the workshops are also presented.

246. Galvin, Thomas J. and Shaffer, Kenneth R. "Special Report:

A Dissertationless Library Doctorate at Simmons

College." Wilson Library Bulletin. 48 (November

1973), 207-09.

In September, 1973 the School of Library Science at
Simmons College inaugurated a new Doctor of Arts degree
program planned especially for practicing librarians who
have work experience at the middle management level.

Simmons followed the recommendation of Kortendick and
Stone in their study of federal librarians that advanced
training in the skills of administration and supervision
should represent an area of highest priority in the design
of new continuing education programs.

Dragout and dropout at the doctoral level, along with
repeated questioning of the relevance of the dissertation,
have led to a marked surge of current interest in alternative degree programs.

Candidates must have an M.L.S. degree and a subject
master's. The Simmons program focuses specifically on
the specialized administrative knowledge directly
applicable to the operational concerns of libraries.

The authors provide additional information on application procedures and cost.

247. Grindeland, W. D. "Tackling the New Through a District

IMC." [Instructional Materials Center]. Wisconsin

Library Bulletin. 64 (July 1968), 251-52.

The Division of Instructional Services, serving
Unified School District Number 1 in Racine County,
Wisconsin, conducts an annual in-service program for
teachers, librarians, and principals. The division has
consultants in all subject areas who teach materials
selection in five sessions of three hours each. One of

the "courses" offered is instructional media. The library
and the audiovisual services are one. The librarian of
the future will need training in both these areas.

248. Haas, Joyce H. and Kreamer, Katherine A. Narrative

Evaluation Report on the Institute for Training in

Librarianship: The Librarian in a Pluralist Society:

Cross-Cultural Training for Social Action. Report

from the University of Hawaii, Honolulu, August,

1971-May, 1972. 113p. ED 075 059.

Twenty-one librarians and ten students were enrolled
in a nine month program in cross-cultural training. The
purpose of the institute was to implement an experimental
program for library personnel relevant to the quality of
library service to the disadvantaged; evaluate the results
of that program; and develop a specialized minor within
the library school curriculum based on that evaluation.
Emphasized in the program were involvement in planning
and evaluation of the program, intensive training in
cross-cultural communication, and an introduction to
field experience with social agencies and social programs,
and others.

249. Hall, Anna C. "An Experiment in Continuing Education for

Professional Librarians." Pennsylvania Library

Association Bulletin. 26 (March 1971), 92-96.

The Carnegie Library of Pittsburgh held a continuing
education program to train top-level personnel to participate in short- and long-range planning, policy-making
and budgeting. The results of an evaluation of the
subject content and the course structure are presented.

250. Hartje, George N. <u>Teaching Library Science and Tele-</u>

      <u>lecture</u>. Columbia, Missouri: University of

      Missouri Graduate School of Library and Information

      Science, 1973. 10p. ED 075 049.

      Amplified voice telephone was used as a form of
telelecture in a library science class at the University
of Missouri. The students communicated with an academic
library administrator and found the experience of value.
The technical details of this instructional media technique are also discussed.

251. Hiatt, Peter. "Continuing Education and PNLA." <u>PNLA</u>

      <u>Quarterly</u>. 37 (Spring 1973), 10-16.

      The Pacific Northwest Library Association began a
four year experiment in 1970 to build all programs around
continuing education activities. The first three years
of the project are discussed with special emphasis on
an evaluation of the third year. The Western Interstate Commission for Higher Education (WICHE) evaluated
PNLA's first total continuing education conference. Participants' responses to the workshops are given. Some
conclusions made by WICHE are that members' involvement
in the planning, conducting, and evaluating of their own
programming makes for more meaningful programs. A
carefully thought out planning process results in better
programs. Personnel from all types of libraries are
represented, resulting in cross-type library participation. WICHE recommends that PNLA continue to urge
continuing education for its members, encourage needs
assessment activities for future program topics, and
attempt to involve a greater representation of school librarians and public library trustees.

252. Hiatt, Peter. "Continuing Education for Librarians in

Indiana." Focus. 21 (June 1967), 57-62.

Public and academic libraries as well as the State
Library in Indiana sponsor formal and informal continuing
education opportunities around the state. A sampling of
the programs is listed in table form. Data for each
program include the name of the sponsoring agency,
objectives, date and location of the program, and requirements for participation.

253. Hinchliff, W. E. "Staff Development: Key to Library

Progress." Wisconsin Library Bulletin. 63 (January

1967), 30-32.

The author describes both the formal and informal
types of staff development activities offered by the
Milwaukee Public Library to its staff.

254. Holzbauer, Herbert. "Inhouse ADP Training." Special

Libraries. 58 (July-August 1967), 427-28.

The Department of the Interior Library decided to
train its staff to utilize electronic data processing
applications which were to be installed in the library.
Although such courses were available in the Washington, D.
area, the library decided to provide in-house training for
the following reasons.

The program could be designed around the mechanics
of the library's own situation during the changeover.
The problems would be realistic since the staff were
familiar with internal procedures. Another reason was
that each staff member could take the training course
and still keep up with daily responsibilities of his job.

The article further describes the course of study
and the academic achievement of the staff-students.

255. Hutchinson, Helen D. "Personnel Administration: In-

service Training at the Nonprofessional Level."

Medical Library Association Bulletin. 53 (October

1965), 542-45.

Library administrators in all types of libraries are
re-evaluating exactly what constitutes professional work.
The Free Library of Philadelphia has developed formal
position classifications providing for the hiring of non-
librarians in positions once classified as professional
as well as the usual clerical assignments. The library
staff accept these classifications. The article outlines
the training plan for nonprofessionals developed by the
Free Library.

256. Janaske, Paul C. "OE's Institutes Program." Library

Journal. 93 (September 1, 1969), 2972-74.

This is a summary report on the current program of
institutes for training in librarianship under Title II-B
of the Higher Education Act, and on the plans for fiscal
year 1969.

The subject matter of the institutes is varied; of
the 66 institutes held, 29 programs dealt with school
librarianship; others were concerned with map librarianship, government publications, oral history, and others.

The Policies and Procedures Manual of the U.S.
Office of Education includes detailed instructions for
submitting proposals for possible institutes in continuing
education.

257. Klassen, Robert. "Institutes for Training in Librarian-

ship: Summer 1969 and Academic Year 1969/1970."

Special Libraries. 60 (March 1969), 185-89.

This is a listing of continuing education institutes funded by the Federal Government in 1969. The institutes were directed towards the needs of special librarians and information science personnel.

Topics range over several subjects--interpersonal relations in libraries, middle management in the library, and library systems analysis and design.

258.　"Leadership Training Institute." American Libraries.

5 (March 1974), 150.

The Leadership Training Institute (LTI) is an Office of Education Project funded under HEA Title II-B and directed by Dr. Harold Goldstein of Florida State University. Unlike most institutes, LTI has no scheduled academic program. Its purpose is to identify library leadership training needs and to provide assistance and coordination to the institutes for training in librarianship also funded under HEA Title II-B.

A two-day workshop was held on "Training for Library Service in the 70s--The Role of Library Associations." Several issues were discussed--"How can library leaders anticipate the social, political, and technological force bringing change to the profession in the next five years and provide updated continuing education programs? What is the role of library associations in exchanging information, designing training programs, and creating incentives?"

259.　Markel, J. Louise. "Training the New Employee." SLA

Sci-Tech News. 21 (Summer 1967), 34-35+. (reprinte

from Radiations. 12 (no. 1, 1966).

The Oak Ridge Associated Universities Library has a systematic program for training new employees. During the job interview, the prospective candidate is given a brief resume of the organization and of the vacancy, and speaks with the staff. Initial impressions by both parties are important. Once the person is hired, the supervisor discusses procedural policies of the library and acquaints him with other staff members. The supervisor discusses specific responsibilities, allows the new employee to develop his own work habits and methods as long as they do not conflict greatly with established routines, and gives full explanation of the rationale behind administrative procedures, applicable to the employee's responsibilities. Each new employee is given time to form a general picture of each library function. A common problem for the supervisor is to expect too much too soon. The employee needs time to absorb the information he is learning and lessen his anxiety about his job performance.

260. Martin, J. A. "Postgraduate-Training Program for Science

Librarians: A Six-Year Review." Medical Library

Association Bulletin. 61 (October 1973), 396-99.

The University of Tennessee Medical Units has a postgraduate training program for science librarians under a grant from the National Library of Medicine. This report includes personal interview and questionnaire results from twenty-five graduate trainees, fifteen scientist advisors, and present employers. All trainees had advanced degrees in library science. They worked with senior scientists as integral members of research teams in laboratories. Trainees responded that the experience gave them a better comprehension of the library needs of the scientists. All but one of the twenty-seven trainees said he would recommend the training program to others.

261. Medical Library Association News. "Continuing Education

Opportunities Available." Medical Library Association

News. 50 (February 1974), 6.

262. "Missouri State Library Stages Cultural Briefings for

     Public Library Administrators." Library Journal.

     93 (January 15, 1968), 138+.

     About fifty administrators of public libraries par-
ticipated in week-long sessions concerning the library's
responsibility in broad areas of contemporary intellectual concern. Prominent authorities spoke in the areas
of fine arts, current issues, and science. This is the
third year for the program funded by the Missouri State
Library.

263. Mitchell, Betty Jo. "In-house Training of Supervisory

     Library Assistants in a Large Academic Library."

     College and Research Libraries. 34 (March 1973),

     144-49.

     The need for in-house supervisory programs is pre-
sented as well as the results of a program undertaken at
one institution. The program has proven to be a successful tool for improving the skills of supervisors. The
first year's experiences also underscore the need to
explain the program's goals to staff at the beginning.

264. Monroe, Margaret E. "AIM: An Independent Study Program

     in Library Science." Journal of Education for

     Librarianship. 6 (Fall 1965), 95-102.

     This paper outlines an independent study program in
library science entitled Articulated Instructional Media
(AIM). The Extension Division of the University of
Wisconsin developed selected instructional media into
units for independent study accessible off-campus but
worthy of on-campus credit. The AIM course includes programmed learning materials. Evaluation of the students'

success will be based on standard tests to measure general
ability, final course content examination, and a test of
professional attitudes and commitments. These tests will
be given to both on-campus and off-campus students of the
Core Course Program.

265. "NLW Exchange Day." American Libraries. 5 (April 1974),

178.

National Library Week (NLW) is being observed in
Bloomington, Indiana with a unique one-day exchange of librarians on the staff of the Monroe County Public Library
and members of the faculty of the Indiana University
Graduate Library School. One purpose is that librarians
trade jobs to learn more about the responsibilities and
problems confronting each other. The program will also
provide increased contact between graduate school students
and practicing librarians. The project may be extended
beyond National Library Week.

266. "Opportunities for All: Continuing Education." Library

Journal. 99 (October 1, 1974), 2439.

This article features several workshops on continuing
education programs. One in Maryland is of particular
interest. A scholarship program has been set up under
the auspices of the Maryland Library Association to
enable working professional and nonprofessional library
staff to advance professionally through part-time college
courses.

267. "Opportunities for Continuing Informal Library Education

in Wisconsin." Wisconsin Library Bulletin. 63

(January 1967), 14-24.

Seven brief articles present some approach to continuing education. The first lists the types of informal education opportunities in table form. Objectives for each program and the participating agency are given. Other articles discuss planning for in-service training, the Wisconsin Valley training program, continuing education for librarians through the university extension, institutes for public libraries, school library workshops and institutes, and the Cooperative Children's Book Center's function in training.

268. Parker, Edna G. "The Art of Helping." Alabama Librarian.

23 (Winter 1972), 25-26.

The Phenix City-Russell County Library staff conducted a series of lessons in basic instruction in library service for community librarians in the area. The series, "The Art of Helping," was aired over ETV (Educational Television). Each program dealt with basic library procedures, the use of library materials and resources, and assisting patrons in the use of library materials. Public and school librarians and library aides were contacted and given time to view the programs. Bookmobile librarians also arranged hours so they could participate. County library staff members prepared assignments and arranged lecture-discussions in weekly follow-up sessions. Study materials and visual aids were also employed. There was a total attendance of eighteen community librarians.

269. Pings, Vern M. and Cruzat, Gwendolyn S. An Assessment of

a Post-Master's Internship in Biomedical Librarian-

ship. Detroit: Wayne State University, Biomedical

Information Center, 1970. 48p. ED 046 426.

The Wayne State University Medical Library conducted a post-master's training program from 1967-1970. An evaluation of the program is given here. Several conclusions are made: 1) a one-year post-master's program

is too short a time for students to learn planning and
management tasks for libraries; 2) a post-master's program should not teach basic library skills; 3) for an
internship program to be justified, students should
learn to apply theoretical knowledge in a working
environment in a specialty or they should learn the
operations of a large library with the expectation of
employment; and 4) an internship provides the working
environment so that librarians can understand how biomedical information is generated and used.

270. Reed, Sarah R. "Education Activities of Library Associa-

tions." Drexel Library Quarterly. 3 (October

1967), 375-90.

Library associations have a continuing responsibility
to see that quality library education programs are available in the area served and that members are encouraged
to avail themselves of such opportunities. This article
totals and describes the programs for continuing education sponsored by library associations in each state
in a three-year period as well as programs offered by the
national library associations.

271. Reed, Sarah R., ed. Continuing Education for Librarians--

Conferences, Workshops and Short Courses, 1964-1965.

Washington, D.C.: Office of Education, U.S. Depart-

ment of Health, Education and Welfare. 1964.

272. Reed, Sarah R., ed. Continuing Education for Librarians--

Conferences, Workshops and Short Courses, 1966-1967.

Washington, D.C.: Office of Education, U.S. Depart-

ment of Health, Education and Welfare. 1966.

273. Reed, Sarah R. and Toye, Willie P., comps. Continuing Education for Librarians: Conferences, Workshops, and Short Courses, 1965-66. United States Education Office. Library Services Branch. 33p.

274. Rink, Bernard C. "Continuing Education for Library Personnel." Michigan Librarian. 38 (Spring 1972), 2+

Mr. Rink outlines the role of the Michigan Library Association in statewide continuing education of library personnel. Major activities include several workshops around the state and association meetings.

275. Scanland, Jackie. "USC (University of South Carolina) Summer Institute for Advance Study in Library Science." South Carolina Librarian. 11 (October 1966), 15-17.

The University of South Carolina featured a six-week institute on "The School Library as a Materials Center." Its purpose was to teach practicing librarians to be more versatile in the selection of materials for students involved in independent study. Librarians from elementary, junior, and senior high schools were represented. Each participant wrote a proposal for the organization and administration of a learning resource center at his or her school.

276. Sheldon, Brooke E., ed. Planning and Evaluating Library Training Programs: A Guide for Library Leaders, Staffs and Advisory Groups. Tallahassee: Florida State University, School of Library Science, The Leadership Training Institute, 1973. 61p.

Funded by USOE, HEA, Title II-B, the Leadership Training Institute provides selected training activities to fill the gap in library leadership training. Library institute directors, faculty, and key library and media personnel identified needs and problems in the area. A frequent area of concern was planning and evaluation. This report is based on information obtained at three training sessions on evaluation conducted in 1973 for Institute directors and staff. The planning and evaluation model used was CIPP (Context, Input, Process, Product), which allowed for on-going evaluation and the specifying of measurable objectives during the project. The CIPP Model is discussed in detail. Delayne Hudspeth writes on "Delphi Forecasting for Long Range Planning; Ken Eye and Jerry Walker discuss "Twenty Tips on Evaluation from the Professional."

277. "Statewide Video Training for Wisconsin Librarians."

Library Journal. 99 (October 15, 1974), 2564.

Wisconsin's Division for Library Services has launched an intensive statewide project aimed at training public librarians in video programming and developing a cooperative videotape exchange program among libraries. The one-year program which has been funded under a $33,500 LSCA grant, will be handled by the Coordinated Library Information Program (CLIP).

The new program will start off with basic training in the use of equipment and script writing in individual libraries and library systems around the state. It will result in regular video programming production and interlibrary exchange of videotapes between Wisconsin libraries and interested libraries across the nation.

278. "Summer Internship." California Librarian. 26 (January

1965), 50.

The California State Library offered ten summer internships for undergraduate college students who were interested in a career in librarianship. The internships were intended to develop and improve library service in

public libraries as well as introduce students to the
field of librarianship.

279. "Training of Branch Library Staff Los Angeles Public

   Library." Library Trends. 14 (April 1966), 410-11.

   An organizational chart is presented of the responsibilities of the supervisor or training agency in the
in-service training and orientation for the professional
and nonprofessional staff.

280. "Tulsa Brings Sociologist into In-service Training."

   Library Journal. 93 (May 15, 1968), 1952.

   The Tulsa City-County Library System conducted a
workshop course entitled "Personnel Relations in Library
Management" for its staff. Tulsa brings in professionals
from other disciplines such as sociology to assist librarians to view their problems with a broad perspective.
The workshop employed the techniques of sensitivity
training and personnel management.

281. "Two New Probrams at ISL." American Libraries. 5

   (November 1974), 537.

   The Illinois State Library is sponsoring a Shared
Staffing Grant Program. A professional librarian will
be shared among two or three libraries in small communities that cannot afford professional library staff.

   The second program concerns continuing education.
Six grant awards will be made annually for three years.
These fellowships are to provide career employees the
opportunity for advance educational programs for advanced
and non-degree-related study. The major emphasis of this
fellowship program will be on problem solving for concerns of state and national level interest. The study
must be related to improved public library service and
not for academic, special, or school libraries alone.

282. Vaillancourt, Pauline M. and Whalen, Lucille. "Special

Libraries Cooperate to Promote an Internship Program."

Special Libraries. 64 (November 1973), 493-97.

This article provides a brief history of the
philosophy concerning the value of "field work" as part
of a formal library school curriculum. Since the 1930's
field work experience has received very little attention
in library literature.

The School of Library and Information Science, State
University of New York at Albany combined the theoretical
and practical approaches in giving students an internship
course and a special seminar simultaneously. Librarians
in eight special libraries in the Albany area cooperated
with the library school faculty in setting up an internship program. The faculty member was responsible for
coordinating, evaluating, and grading the student's work.
Two courses were offered in conjunction with the internships that related to the working experience. The
students and the participating libraries found the
experience worthwhile.

283. Walker, H. Thomas. "In-service Training for Subprofes-

sionals." ALA Bulletin. 59 (Fall 1965), 134-38.

The Division of Library Extension, Maryland State
Department of Education, began an in-service training
course for selected employees of county public libraries.
This article recounts the progress of the program.
Students are trained for limited responsibility under
continuous supervision by a professional librarian. The
training is designed for specific jobs. It is a stop-gap
training program of twenty weeks; it does not aim to
promote employees into professional positions. Program
content is outlined as well as the evaluation used.

284. Wender, Ruth W. "Training Small Hospital Library Personnel

by the Preceptorship Method." 64 (September 1973),

370-73.

The University of Oklahoma Health Sciences Center
Library has a practical approach to the improvement of
medical information systems in small hospitals. The
trainees, usually medical record department members, are
untrained in library methods even though they are charged
with the supervision of a library. These people are
trained as library managers through a preceptorship experience in two medical libraries with the loan of a demonstration collection of basic books and indexes to the
journal literature and a vigorous on-site consultation
program.

285. Zachert, Martha Jane K., and Sursa, Mary Lou. "Continuing

Education for Librarianship: Evaluation of SLA's

1969 Seminars." Special Libraries. 60 (November

1969), 616-17.

For the first time the Special Libraries Association
presented four concurrent seminars on personnel administration, planning the library facility, problem publications,
and basic principles of management. The programs were
held during the 1969 Conference. The majority of participants found the seminars worthwhile and would be
willing to pay to attend future continuing education programs.

PART II

Continuing Professional Education in
Librarianship in Other Countries

A. Theory and Philosophy

286. Beacock, E. Stanley. "View of Continuing Education of Li-

brarians by an Employer." IPLO Quarterly. [Institute

of Professional Librarians of Ontario.] 14 (October

1972), 66-70.

In this article, the author makes several cogent
observations concerning continuing education of professional librarians. He argues that to date not only in
Canada but in the U.S. as well, both employees and administrators have evidenced little interest in continuing
education for librarians. Further, library schools and
professional library organizations have done little to provide such opportunities. For example, no library school in
Canada has a person in charge of university extension. To
change this status quo, pressure must come from groups of
librarians working in concert to force administrators to
plan programs and grant release time and tuition benefits.

287. Bewley, Lois M. "To Educate Ourselves Continuously."

British Columbia Library Quarterly. 33 (July-

October 1969), 23-25.

The author asks several questions to which there are
as yet few answers. When librarians refer to continuing
education are we considering, need, adequacy of current
activity, program content, demand, response, cost, organization, and recognition? All are essential components of a
program of continuing education. A sound program of continuing education must provide sustained, high calibre,
accessible, professionally oriented learning opportunities
sponsored by an agency or group recognized by the employer,
and reflected in measurable improvement in the performance
of the staff.

288. Bone, Larry E., ed. Library Education: An International

Survey. Papers presented at the International Confer-

ence on Librarianship, June 12-16, 1967. Champaign,

Illinois: University of Illinois. Graduate School

of Library Science, 1968. 388p.

Aspects of library education are grouped under five
main themes: 1) an historical picture of education for
librarianship is given tracing the evolution of professiona
library education in the United States, South America,
Continental Europe, and Great Britian; 2) the organization
and operation of library schools as well as curriculum
principles and practices; 3) teaching methods in library
education; 4) the nature of research and research activities in library schools throughout the world; and 5) the
roles that the national and international library associations have played in library education.

289. Böttcher, W. "Wie Geht es in der Weiterbildung Weiter."

(How Does Continuing Education Progress?) Bibliotekar

19 (July 1965), 683-85.

This article describes the problems the East German
Government has encountered in planning a specialized continuing education program. The Government's goal is to
develop a unified library system throughout the country,
and to train librarians in subject specialties. Problems
exist in establishing the depth of specialization necessary
for adequate technical support in libraries. No decision
has yet been made as to how these programs should be
implemented. There is a discussion of the value of a postgraduate curriculum with definite course content and the
awarding of a certification upon completion of the program.

290. Colley, D. I. "Training: The Theoretical Background."

   Library Association Record. 72 (November 1970), 349-50.

   Any training program should consider the needs of
employees and the responsibilities of management. Employees
are motivated to accept and seek responsibility and show
initiative when the organization they work for satisfies
their needs. While attending in-service training programs,
employees of Manchester (England) Public Libraries ranked
their expectations of the library in which they were
employed. The highest ranked items are: to have an
interesting job; to experience a sense of achievement; to
have opportunities for promotion and growth; and, to receive full appreciation for work performed. The four
lowest ranked items in terms of importance are: to have a
secure job; to be kept in the picture; to be on good terms
with the supervisor; and to work for as few hours as
possible.

291. Davinson, D. E. "Short Courses for Qualified Librarians."

   New Library World. 73 (July 1971), 14-15.

   This article discusses the possible reasons why librarians have low attendance at short courses. In the
author's opinion efficient planning, both of content and
of locale, would contribute to more successful programs.

292. Dean, J. R. "Senior Staff Training--An Approach."

   Library World. 70 (June 1969), 339-41.

   In Great Britain, the introduction of full-time courses
for librarianship has created a situation where libraries
are appointing senior assistants (recent library school
graduates) with little or no actual library experience.
Although library schools give students some exposure to
libraries in the course curriculum, the Library Association
requires that persons have at least one year's approved
full-time library service after completing a comprehensive

examination. The author describes what is being done in
his library system to resolve the problem. Job rotation
and role playing are some of the approaches employed.

293. Dickson, Lance E. "American Library Education for South

African Librarians." South African Libraries.

41 (October 1973), 77-82.

The richest resources for continuing education of professional librarians in the United States are the regular
semester courses of instruction offered to students in
library schools. While the South African librarian can
acquire a quality master's degree in library science in his
own country, U.S. library schools offer several advantages
for professional development: 1) some library schools are
housed in great academic libraries with a wealth of book
collections for research; 2) the results of an almost
totally uncensored literary environment may be directly
observed; 3) the opportunity to come into contact with
other librarians representing several countries; and 4) a
more informal method of class instruction than is to be
found in South Africa. The author lists titles of directo-
ries and handbooks to which interested librarians may
refer for further information on types of courses offered
and admission requirements of library schools.

294. Harrison, J. C. "INTAMEL, International Meeting,

Gothenburg, 1969: Staff Training in Large City Li-

braries." International Library Review. 1 (October

1969), 475-78.

Staff training is essential because of the increasing
complexity of services. Courses should be arranged for
newly-qualified librarians joining the system and for older
librarians in need of refresher courses. Needed are qualified and experienced instructors, the full cooperation of
all the staff, and suitable accommodations and aids.
Specific topics are outlined.

295. Harrison, J. Clement. "Advanced Study: A Mid-Atlantic

Point of View." In: Larry E. Bone, ed. Library

Education: An International Survey. Champaign,

Illinois: University of Illinois Graduate School of

Library Science, 1968. pp. 329-36.

Most American (U.S.) librarians think "advanced study"
means study toward a doctoral degree. The role of the
Advanced Certificate awarded by some library schools for
post-master's study demands more attention. The certificate
offers an opportunity for some form of specialization not
handled at the master's level and not requiring the rigor
of the dissertation at the doctoral level. The certificate
must not be considered a limbo for those not accepted into
doctoral programs but must have a life of its own, properly
organized and directed towards clearly indicated objectives
such as information science specialization, international
librarianship (which would include foreign language study),
or preparation for teaching. Advanced study will play its
part if its objectives are determined beforehand, if it is
coordinated with the basic programs and, if the schools are
able to provide adequate resources in terms of faculty and
materials.

The "multi-level" approach to education for librarianship in a number of European countries is also described.

296. Hogue, M. B. "From Books to Benefits." Australian

Academic and Research Libraries. 2 (September 1971),

116-22.

The University Library of New South Wales has compiled
a list of twelve pamphlets to be used in its in-service
training program. The most difficult tasks are to determine the relative value of the materials and to measure
the results of any in-service training course. The author,
training librarian at the University, discusses the content

and organization of the pamphlets; he concludes that they are directed toward new staff members, both professional and non-professional. Industry has successfully used cost-benefit analysis to measure the effectiveness of in-service training programs. While libraries do not have simple profit or loss as their final measure, seven factors can be considered to measure cost. Each of the seven factors is described. The purpose of in-service training of all staff is to produce individuals who know about the library, its operations, and the role they play in it.

297. Immelman, R. F. M. "Continuing Education of Library

Personnel." South African Libraries. 37 (December

1969), 128-43.

In addition to discussing continuing education, the Director of the School of Librarianship of the University of Cape Town also refers specifically to a work-study scheme, in-service training, internship, and librarian-trainees. He cites examples of application of each of the above approaches especially those attempted in the United States and Great Britain.

298. Ingham, Margaret. "The Professional Development of the

Children's Librarian." In: Library Association of

Australia. Conference, 1971, Sidney. Proceedings.

1972. pp. 325-36.

Implicit in the term "professional development" is the concept of continuing education of librarians after they have completed their basic studies and have been certified. Professional development of children's librarians is addressed specifically as well as the ingredients necessary to provide motivation for continuing education. Also examined is the state of continuing education in the United States, Canada, Great Britain and Australia. Specific emphasis is given to Australia regarding recommendations for improvement in the standards and status of children's librarianship.

299. Klompen, W. "Überlegungen zur Bibliothekarischen Fortbildung

    für Dozenten." (Thoughts on Continuing Library Educa-

    tion of Library School Teachers). In: Bibliotheksarbeit

    Heute. Frankfurt am Main, Klostermann, 1973. p. 68-73).

300. Krieg, W. "Fortbildung der Bibliothekare an Öffentlichen

    Bücherein." (Continuing Education of Librarians in

    Public Libraries). Bücherei und Bildung. 17

    (February 1965), 65-67.

301. Lee, Robert and Lee, Charlene Swarthout. "Personnel

    Planning for a Library Manpower System." Library

    Trends. 20 (July 1971), 19-38.

    Presented is an overview of the nature of the per-
sonnel planning system of the Western Ontario Library,
Canada. This approach is concerned with the management
of all the human resources in the library system. The
manpower, development, and recruitment plans all have
systematic, in-depth approaches for developing good, long-
term, personnel planning. Human potential is emphasized.
Staff participate in the process resulting in higher job
satisfaction and increased productivity. The standard
used in measuring the growth of a personnel development
plan is the degree of success of the organization (the
library) to satisfy the personal goals of the individuals
in the organization. Three principles of participatory
management are described: 1) personal worth and importance
is built upon work experience; 2) the supervisor is held
accountable for all decisions, their execution, and their
results; and 3) each staff member has high performance
aspirations.

302. "Leeds' Continuing Ed. Degree Approved by the CNAA."

    Library Journal. 99 (September 15, 1974), 2114.

    England's Council for National Academic Awards has approved a degree proposal, submitted by Leeds Polytechnic Department of Librarianship, calling for the creation of a part-time graduate-level course for senior librarians. Librarians can earn the new degree (M.A.) upon completion of two or three years of part-time study. The course will be offered in January of next year. Approval for the new course, said the University, "marks the culmination of a five-year development plan embarked upon in 1970... to create a structure of full-time, part-time, and short courses together with a program of research work designed to give the department a fully comprehensive range of courses and programs."

303. Lewis, David T. "In-service Training: A New Dimension."

    New Library World. 73 (July 1971), 20-21.

    Lewis recommends an interchange between practicing librarians and library schools as an effective means of continuing education. Forms such an interchange might take include joint courses in practical aspects of the profession, librarians without degrees enrolling in degree courses, and one-day symposia.

304. Library Association. Youth Libraries Group. "Post-

    Examination Training for Children's Librarianship."

    Library Association Record. 72 (March 1970), 106-07.

    A committee of the Youth Libraries group of the Library Association in Great Britain outlines several recommendations for children's librarianship. The committee assesses the current status of training for children's librarians. Recommendations for post-examination training are given for the newly qualified librarian: training program, training librarians from other departments (e.g., adult services, technical services), cooperative training schemes; and the designation of training officers.

305. Miller, Vivian. "Trends in Toronto Public Library Staff

Training and Development." Ontario Library Review.

52 (March 1968), 17-18.

A total training program must include three areas of
focus: 1) a knowledge of the library itself, its history,
government, objectives, problems and procedures, its
physical plant, services, and resources; 2) continuing
development in a specialty either through work with a
sector of the community or with a portion of the library's
resources; and 3) continuing development in operational
or managerial skills. The author briefly outlines how
the three above steps are implemented by the Toronto Public
Library.

306. "Neus System der Weiterbildung," (New System of Continuing

Education). Bibliothekar. 19 (July 1965), 678-83.

Continuing education takes three forms in the state
supported programs in East Germany: 1) on-the-job training
and short courses taught in a library; 2) training sessions
for library personnel in a given city; and 3) nation-wide
continuing education seminars. The plan of the government
is to continue to educate as many people as possible in
the existing school for continuing education in librarianship, offer occasional courses for library administrators,
and hold training sessions for the special problems librarians experience working in large and medium sized libraries. The article describes in detail the content of
courses for specialization in the social sciences, pure
science, and technology. Emphasis is on self instruction
after orientation lectures. Training will include on-site
visits to schools, special libraries, and others. At the
end of each specialization course, there will be a meeting
to summarize material learned and to discuss applications
to library work.

307. Newsom, H. E. "Continuing Education for Librarians." In:

Education for Librarianship. Papers presented at a

workshop, University of Alberta, School of Library

Science, University of Alberta, 1970. pp. 42-53.

No librarian should feel his education is complete
when he has received his basic professional degree. Technological advances and changes in the social structure
mean librarians must also change. Professional renewal
can be brought about by courses in librarianship on an
advanced level, courses in subject fields, extensive workshops, conferences, travel and observation, and profession
literature.

308. Paltridge, Cynthia. "Education and Qualifications for

Librarianship." Proceedings of the 14th Biennial

Conference, Library Association of Australia. 2 (196

516-18.

Children's literature and children's librarians in
Australia do not have the high status that children's librarianship enjoys in the United States. Australian library schools do not have any courses in children's
literature. School librarians take the Registration
Examination at the undergraduate level. The Wark Committe
recommends that librarians ought to be trained in Colleges
of Advanced Education. The author strongly disagrees with
this and states that children's librarians need a knowledg
of children, their interests, and other behavioral and
psychological influences on them. Two recommendations are
made: 1) a system of internship should be set up for
school or public librarians recently graduated from librar
school so that they can work for two years in selected
schools or public libraries before they are in charge of
one; and 2) demonstration libraries (public and school)
should be set up with a high level of staff and book resources serving as practice schools.

309. Pepper, Alan G., ed. <u>Seminar on Training of Community</u>

<u>Librarians, Thunder Bay, Ontario, 1974; Proceedings</u>.

Thunder Bay, Ontario: Northwestern Regional Library

System, 1975. 160p.

The Northwestern Regional Library System sponsored
a seminar from September 30 to October 2, 1974 for librarians from the United States and Canada. The theme
of the program concerned the problems of training library
staff in relatively isolated situations who must carry out
much of their work without the direct supervision of a
professional staff member throughout the less populated
regions of the North American Continent. Four main speakers
addressed specific topics followed by a reactor panel and
group study sessions. Roy Stokes, Director, School of
Librarianship, University of British Columbia, discussed
the part the library school has to play in the training
of community librarians. Cliff Weaver, Coordinator,
Library Technicion Program, Fanshawe College, London,
Ontario, focused on the role of the community colleges in
such training programs. Speaking on behalf of the Province/
State role was Grace Buller, Provincial Library Service,
Toronto, Ontario. Reporting on a community training pro-
gram in operation was Frank Obljubek, Regional Consultant,
Northwestern Regional Library System, Thunder Bay, Ontario.
Other members of the reactor panel were John Marshall,
University of Toronto; Alice Roy, Kansas State Library;
and Helen Netter, Mid-Hudson Library System, Poughkeepsie,
New York.

310. "Post-examination Training for Children's Librarianship."

<u>Library Association Record</u>. 72 (March 1970), 106-07.

This memorandum constitutes the deliberations of a
working party set up by the Committee of the Youth Libraries Group at the County Library in Aylesbury, England.
Recommendations are made concerning training programs,
co-operative training schemes, and the designation of
training officers.

311. Ramsay, Margery. "The Education of Special Groups." In:

Library Association of Australia, Conference, 1969,

Adelaide. Proceedings. Library Association of

Australia. 1971. p. 490-96.

This seminar deals with the education of two types
of individuals in Australia: 1) the isolated student who
does not have easy access to library schools, and 2) the
advanced student or qualified librarian in need of continuing processional education. For the former, there
is a shortage of qualified staff based on statistical data
They do not hold a degree and need to improve their skills
Staffing, recruitment, and conditions of employment of
isolated students are discussed. For advanced level
students in the second category, the realization of professional librarians for further education has grown in
Australia in the last few years. Reasons for this growth
are listed. Types of continuing education programs to
meet these needs in Australia are covered.

312. Standley, A. E. "Part-time Education in Librarianship:

A Continuing Need." Library Association Record.

72 (March 1970), 91-92.

The author proposes that librarianship should be the
general term to describe all librarianship and informatio
activities. Education for librarianship should be examin
as a whole.

There is a continuing need for part-time education
and training, particularly in non-public libraries. To
meet this need, part-time library education centers shoul
be set up with support from the Department of Education
and Science of the British Government. Full-time schools
and all librarianship organizations can provide part-time
and short courses in a planned, systematic way. The
centers should be situated at the most central point
possible in a limited number of very high population area

313. Stokes, Roy B. "The Road Ahead?" British Columbia Library

Quarterly. 37 (Summer-Autumn 1973), 5-16.

Professor Stokes discusses whether librarianship can be considered a profession and if it is, what the education of such an individual should involve. He recommends that applicants who wish to enter library school must first have a year's work experience in a library. This would entail organized, year-long, in-service training in libraries. The aspirant would be exposed to the library profession as a whole, not just to the methods of operation of one department. This process would allow individuals to experience the field and decide whether they want to continue the profession as a career.

The library science curriculum at the University of British Columbia School of Librarianship is also discussed. Two weeks are devoted to in-service training for first year library school students. However, this is a brief exposure. There is still not sufficient continuing contact between the library school and the profession at large.

314. Thauer, W. "Weiterbildungs--und Büchereigesetz in

Baden-Württemberg Vorerst Zurückgestellt."

(Continuing Education and Library Legislation in

Baden-Württemberg postponed for the Time Being).

Buch und Bibliothek. 23 (November-December 1971), 1144.

City officials in Baden-Wurttemberg (West Germany) want a law enacted that would require continuing education for librarians and suggested such action to the cultural ministry in July, 1971. This proposal is not being acted upon at the present time because sufficient funding is not available to finance such a program.

315. Wassner, H. "DBV/VBB-Fortbildungs-Kommission Arbeitsberic

    Stand: Mai 1971." (DBV/VBB Continuous Education

    Commission; Work Report as of May 1971). B̈uch und

    Bibliothek. 23 (September 1971), 905-08.

    In West Germany an attempt is being made to localize
continuing education rather than to have training on a
national level. Basic standards for the training program
have not yet been set up. To solve this problem, the
author suggests an office of continuing education within
the National Library organization. Local organizations
would inform the main office twice a year concerning
progress they have made in continuing education activities
There would be a yearly evaluation published in a professional journal outlining progress, course content, and
goals of continuing education programs.

316. Weeraperuma, Susunaga. The Role of Conferences in the

    Further Education of Librarians: A Scrutiny of the

    Present Situation with Proposals for Reform. London

    The Author, 1971. 32p. ED 051 832.

    The primary responsibility of the librarian is his
custodianship of books and therefore of culture and knowl
edge. He must maintain surveillance of the most pro-
gressive means of making this knowledge available. Also,
he must keep in touch with developments in his own specia
and related fields. Unfortunately, library science liter
ture does not reflect extensive examination of continuing
education. Offered herein is a systematic presentation o
one facet of the librarian's post-professional education
which is furthered through clinics, group work, conferenc
lectures, institutes, symposia, staff meetings, and workshops, whether national or international. The meaning of
each of these terms is defined and placed in the context
of the librarian's need for continuing education. Advantages and disadvantages of each approach are given.
Suggestions are offered for organizing and running confer
ences on continuing education as well as a listing of the
steps involved in setting up a center for the promotion o
librarians' continuing education.

B. In-Service Training

317. Fox, John. "Newbattle '68: Report on the S.L.A. (Scottish

Library Association) Summer School." SLA News. 86

(July 1968), 126-28.

The article recounts a continuing education seminar
held at Newbattle Abbey during Summer 1968. Lectures
covered several topics on library management: "Development in Education for Librarianship," "Management and
Leadership Style," and "Management Problems."

318. Gimbel, Henning and others. "Betaenkning Vedrørende Kursus

for Biblioleksassistenter ved Folkebibliotekerne."

(Report on Courses for Library Assistants in Public

Libraries). Bogens Verden. 47 (September 1965),

331-44. (Danish publication)

319. Green, S. John. "Newbattle '69: Report on the SLA

(Scottish Library Association) Summer School."

SLA News. 92 (July 1969), 336-39.

Each year the Scottish Library Association sponsors a
summer school program for professional librarians in some
aspect of library science. Guest lecturers, who are
experts in their respective fields, discuss topics. This
year (1969) the syllabus outlined a subject area to be
covered each day, have the experts lecture on the topic,
and then allow full discussion of these ideas. The themes
for this program were: education and training of librarians,
computer applications in libraries, progress in library research, problems in book provision, and libraries and audiovisual education.

320. "Information Über Weiterbildungsmassnahmen für Hauptberufl

   Bibliothekarisch Tätige Mitarbeiter der Allgemeinen

   Öffentlichen Bibliotheken, Gewerkschaftsbibliotheken

   und bibliotheken in den Häusern der Jungen Pioniere."

   (Information on Measures for Continuing Education of

   Full-time Librarians in General Public Libraries,

   Trade Union Libraries and Libraries in Young Pioneer

   Club Houses). Bibliothekar. 20 (November 1966),

   1170-72.

   Courses offered by the East German Government are
   divided into general and specific areas of instruction.
   There is heavy emphasis on instruction in Marxism and
   Leninism as it relates to the understanding and functionin
   of the library in the community. Library education per se
   includes topics such as bibliography, evaluation of materials, planning the library to serve a specific communit
   Classes are on-going so that a participant may complete
   material in certain areas from year to year. There is a
   permanent state building with dormitory facilities for
   extended courses. Participation in these programs is
   required for promotion to higher levels of library administration. Instruction is given in bibliography,
   documentation, community planning, current literature
   (fiction and non-fiction), and critical assessment.

321. Isaacs, Julian M. "In-service Training for Reference

   Work." Library Association Record. 71 (October

   1969), 301-02.

   The author, a technical reference librarian, presents
   a training method used in the commercial and technical
   reference department of a public library which could be

applied to other libraries. The method involves personally
supervised training and assessment, and the use of examples
dealing with different kinds of reference queries.

322. Labdon, Peter. "Re-training for Senior Librarians."

Library Association Record. 68 (February 1966), 42-44.

This is a description of the West Midlands (England)
re-training scheme based on a program dealing with the
subject of communications. A central organization is
required by librarians for education, re-training, and
research. The author emphasizes the need for continuing
education for senior librarians so that length of time
on a job does not mean professional stagnation.

323. "Newbattle '70: An Editorial Impression of the S.L.A.

(Scottish Library Association) Summer School."

SLA News. 98 (July 1970), 100-03.

Each summer the Scottish Library Association sponsors a
continuing education program for professional librarians
representing several nations. Topics discussed during the
1970 session were: the practice and problems of in-service
training, the planning and building of libraries, libraries and
the student reader, students, academics, and libraries,
and aspects of a technical library service to specialist
users.

324. Northwestern Regional Library System. Local Librarians

Training Programme. Thunder Bay, Ontario, Canada.

1974. 64p.

This manual is a guide for a training program for
community librarians in Northwestern Ontario who have no
formal library training. Course outlines, specimen
syllabi, examples of work assignments and examples of
cooperation received from other governmental bodies are

included. This publication is unique in the depth of its coverage and quality of instructional backup materials which are available from the system headquarters. The program is designed to fit the needs of the small, rural public librarian. The courses cover administration, reference work, selection of library materials, cataloging and classification. The program is approximately three years in length and involves lectures, discussion, and assigned homework. Upon successful completion of examinations and projects, the participant is granted a Regional Certificate.

325. Obljubek, Frank. "Northwestern's Training Programme for

Local Librarians." Ontario Library Review. 54

(December 1970), 210-13.

The Northwestern Regional Library System in Thunder Bay, Ontario has developed an effective training program for non-professionals working in small public libraries. Courses are offered in regional locations throughout the system. The main purpose of the program is to help community librarians acquire or improve upon the essential skills of the basic aspects of library work in a small public library. Four courses are offered over a three-year period. Although the program has been in operation for only a year, the director of the training program offers some evaluation of its success. Participation has been high, community librarians are receptive to new ideas, and applications of the procedures taught in the classes are evidenced in some of the libraries. Cost figures are also given.

326. Robertson, Anne. "In-service Training at the Public

Library of New South Wales." Australian Library

Journal. 16 (February 1967), 13-18.

The author is training librarian at the Public Library of New South Wales. She traces the growth of an in-service training scheme, still emerging from its experimental phase, and outlines some of the problems experienced in implementing it.

327. Roder, R. "Das Erste Fortbildungsseminar fur Diplom-

bibliothekare an Offentlichen Bucherein in Nordrhein-

Westfalen." (First Continuing Education Seminar for

Professional Librarians at Public Libraries in North

Rhine-Westphalia). Verband der Bibliotheken des

Landes Nordrhein-Westfalen Mitteilungsblatt.

17 (July 1967), 162-67.

Because of the rapid growth of public libraries and
the lack of trained personnel, the West German Government
sponsored a continuing education program for librarians.
There had been continuing education programs before but
they were few in number and dealt with specialized areas
of librarianship. The four semesters, twenty-one week
program, brought together librarians from all sizes of
public libraries. The number of participants was limited
to twenty-five for an optimum level of discussion. Most
participants had seminar costs paid by their respective
libraries. Some, however, paid their own way if the library was unwilling to defray costs. Topics covered in
the seminar were the library and society, organization of
libraries, collection building, and organization of
materials.

328. Roder, R. "Zweites Fortbildungsseminar Nordrhein-Westfalen."

(Second Seminar for Continuing Education in North

Rhein-Westphalia). Verband der Bibliotheken des

Landes Nordrhein-Westfalen Mitteilungsblatt.

19 (July 1969), 213-15.

The West German Government sponsored a second continu
education program for public librarians. The seminars wer
held for eighteen weekends, once a month in the city of
Essen because of its central location and library facilities. Twenty librarians from medium and large libraries
participated. Topics covered were annotation, cataloging,
computers and printed catalogs, children's literature,
reference, and reader's advisory services.

329. Roob, H. "Zwei Jahre Bibliothekarische Weiterbildung in

Gotha; Ein Erfahrungsbericht." (Two Years of

Continued Professional Training in Librarianship at

Gotha; A Survey of Experience). Zentralblatt fur

Bibliothekswesen. 85 (October 1971), 588-94.

The East German Government sponsors an Institute of
Continuing Professional Education. Its goal is to improve
the quality of work and teaching in East German libraries.
There is a facility for continuing education in Gotha whic
houses as many as twenty-six people for on-site training.
It includes a library, classrooms, dormitory, and dining
room. The training program varies with instruction in
specific library organizational tasks, future planning, an
courses in specific socialist ideological problems. In 19
172 professionals and nonprofessionals participated in
various types of continuing education experiences based on
their individual training and experience.

330. Russell, J. "Training for Librarianship." Library Associ

tion Record. 68 (February 1966), 36-41.

Mr. Russell, coordinator and training officer for the
Manchester Public Libraries in England, summarizes the
results of a survey of library staff. The staff training
course is outlined in Appendix II; Appendix IV details the
new entrants course at major district libraries; Appendice
and VI list advanced staff training in administration and
reader services.

331. Timm, H. "Education Permanente, auch fur Bibliothekare,

    Erstes Fortbildungsseminar auf Bundesebene."

    (Continuous Education for Librarians Too; First

    Educational Seminar on the Federal Level). Bucherei

    und Bildung. 19 (July-August 1967), 421-24.

    There is a necessity for continuing education because
of the rapid growth of knowledge. The goal of the West
German Government is to prepare people for new positions
in libraries. To meet this goal, the government sponsored
its first continuing education seminar. Twenty-four participants met four times at monthly intervals in different
locations throughout the country. This procedure gave
them an overall view of differences in libraries in
West Germany. Guest lecturers spoke on the following
topics: the library as part of the community, internal
library organization, library collection building, and
decision making. The author feels such continuing education experiences should be required every three to five
years so that librarians can keep up-to-date. Reports
on course content will be published later.

332. Yeo, R. "Management Training in North York Public Library."

    Ontario Library Review. 52 (March 1968), 15-16.

    Mr. Yeo, Public Services Coordinator at the North
York Public Library, describes a training program for
supervisory staff at all levels in the area of management.
Session topics are listed. Some are: overcoming resistance to change, creative thinking at all levels, and
improving attitudes of employees toward their jobs.

PART III

Continuing Professional Education in
Other Fields

333. Abrahamson, Stephen and others. Medical Information Proje

A Study of an Audiovisual Device as a Technique for

Continuing Education for Educational Practitioners.

Final Report. Los Angeles: School of Education and

School of Medicine, University of Southern California,

1970. 408p. ED 051 846.

The purpose of the Medical Information Project was
to develop and implement a communication system for
general medical doctors using an individualized, programme
audiovisual medium. The planning involved three phases.
Phase I included a literature survey of medical communication; obtaining a sample of general practitioners; develop
ing instruments to assess doctors' cognitive and affective
reactions; and others. Phase II consisted of distributing
the equipment to the sample of physicians; conducting the
training program for use of the hardware; and pre- and
post-questionnaires and interviews. Phase III covered the
collecting, processing, and analyzing of the data.

334. The City College Workshop Center for Open Education.

1973. 16p. ED 088 862.

The Workshop Center for Open Education was formed on
the basis of the following factors: 1) efforts to con-
struct an alternative to traditional public schools in
New York City had galvanized the interests of hundreds;
2) teachers who had gotten away through the Open Corridor
program needed a place to continue their development; and
3) those trying without advisory support to make first
steps towards open education needed help and reinforcement
Supported by grants from the U.S. Office of Education, the
Ford Foundation, and the Rockefeller Brothers Funds, the
workshop is a new resource for all participants in the
school process--teachers, principals, supervisors, paraprofessionals, parents, and graduate/undergraduate
students--in the New York City area. The Center features

workshop activities ranging from demonstrations to independent work on individual projects and from single or one-time use to continuous or extended use. The facilities include the following: workshops in exploration of materials for curriculum discussions dealing with problems in class and school reorganization; publications that analyze and disseminate information; a darkroom for photography work applicable to classroom uses; and a library for browsing and reference.

335. A Community Project in Religion and Mental Health.

Indianapolis: Indiana University. Medical Center,

1967. 24p. ED 042 080.

From 1964 to 1967 a demonstration program in continuing education for clergy and related professions was sponsored by the National Institute of Mental Health and Lilly Endowment, Inc. Each clergyman received in-service training in utilizing mental health resources in his own community. Administrative centers were located in six areas of Indiana where there were urban, rural, and exurban communities. The areas were Muncie, Fort Wayne, New Castle, Columbus, Lafayette, and a section of Indianapolis. The Indiana University Medical Center held a week's formal orientation for approximately 100 participants. The second week seminars were held concerning individual cases and resources in individual communities. Participants reported on progress and problems every six months. While this approach worked well during the inception of the program, it was recommended that a permanent residential center be established.

336. Gomersall, Earl R. and Myer, M. Scott. "Breakthrough in

On-The-Job Training." Harvard Business Review.

44 (July-August, 1966), 62-72.

The results of a study performed at Texas Instruments Inc. are summarized. The study was concerned with the relationship between organization climate and job performance. One of the purposes was to ascertain what would

occur in a large manufacturing department if the causes fo:
anxiety among new employees were reduced. Job enlargement
was used as a means of countering trends toward regimenta-
tion, social stratification, routine work, and technologica
development. The experiment showed the following gains
because of a reduction in anxiety: training time was
shortened by one-half; training costs were lowered by one-
third; absenteeism and tardiness dropped; waste and
rejects were reduced; and overall costs were cut 15 percent to 30 percent.

337. Goodman, Steven E. National Directory of Adult and Con-

         tinuing Education; A Guide to Programs, Materials, an

         Services. 1968. 285p.

      The recent number of publications, materials, and pro-
grams developed in the field of education and training are
overwhelming. The steady increase has made the task of
locating appropriate instructional materials more difficul
This compilation is to be best utilized as a primary refer
ence book for all persons attempting to locate specialized
programs and materials. The numerous courses, seminars,
and programs cited include those which are available to
personnel in all geographic areas of the United States and
some countries abroad. Libraries are included as are othe:
institutions and agencies.

338. Leonard, Alvin and Parlette, G. Nicholas. Partnership in

         Learning, An Historical Report, 1960-1966.

         San Francisco: American Public Health Association,

         1967. 41p. ED 015 402.

      The western branch of the American Public Health Asso
ciation has a continuing education program for its members
in thirteen states. This report covers the history of the
program from 1960-1966. Seminars and courses deal with

the professional educational needs and covers such topics as health service administration, chronic diseases, mental and environmental health. The report also brings the program up-to-date for 1967. Discussed are its present organization, the status of curriculum development, source of funding and program evaluation.

339. Maddox, Kathryn. "In West Virginia, It Is Working. One

Teacher Education Center in Action." Washington, D.C.:

American Association of Colleges for Teacher Educa-

tion. 1972. 64p. ED 086 679.

This publication explains the concept of the Multi-Institutional Teacher Education Center (MITEC) in Kanawha County, West Virginia. The Center emphasizes the shared responsibility of public schools, communities, students, the state department of education, and colleges in providing continuous professional development of pre- and in-service teachers. Some of the basic tenets found in the MITEC Program are: 1) each participating college and university agrees to orient students to the school district, the Learning Laboratory Centers and MITEC and to develop objective, performance-based evaluation forms for students; 2) continuous evaluation is provided to give new dimensions to the Center's structure; 3) the Advisory Committee agrees on recognition and honoraria for clinical supervising teachers to eliminate competition and discord; and 4) the colleges supervise students in consulting, counseling, and providing in-service programs to MITEC participants. Another facet which is now being implemented at the Center is the sequencing of pre- and in-service teacher education.

340. "Program for Beginning Teachers. An Individualized Ap-

proach to In-Service Education." An Application for

Continuation Grant. Part II. Narrative. 1969. 32p.

ED 036 458.

During its first year of operation eighty first-year teachers from nine public and private elementary schools in the Wilmette suburban district participated in the in-service program in which the individualized program for each teacher was developed by the teacher and one or more staff members. There was a five-day summer workshop and one-half day per month demonstrations, consultation, etc., during the school year. Each participant was teamed with an experienced "helping teacher" who assisted in planning, observation, and self-evaluation.

341. A Symposium on Continuing Medical Education in Montana.

Boulder: Western Interstate Commission for Higher

Education (WICHE), 1969. 23p. ED 033 306.

The Montana Medical Association and the WICHE Mountain States Regional Medical Program sponsored a symposium on continuing medical education in Montana. Several topics were covered: "How Can an Interprofessional Program be Developed?"; "Continuing Medical Education Problems, Priorities, and Plans"; "Can Health Professions Work and Learn Together?"; and "Communication Problems Affecting Patient Care." Other discussions are: "The Development of a Plan for Continuing Medical Education in Montana" and "The Strategy of Interprofessional Continuing Education Development in Montana."

342. Adams, Hobart Warren. <u>In-service Training and Development</u>

<u>Programs for Accountants in Business and Industry</u>.

D.B.A. Thesis. Bloomington: University of Indiana,

1967. 313p. ED 026 613.

A survey was made of in-service training and development for accountants in fifty-three selected business firms
varying in products, sales volume, and employees. Program
philosophy, objectives, qualifications, selection of trainees
and instructors and evaluation procedures were examined.
The major weaknesses of in-service programs lie in training philosophy and evaluative procedures.

343. Adult Education Association of the U.S.A. <u>Federal Support</u>

<u>for Adult Education; A Directory of Programs and</u>

<u>Services</u>. Washington, D.C.: Adult Education, 1966.

111p.

This volume describes the chief agencies that support
adult education programs in any significant way. Much of
this information is dated and may be of little value
because of changing priorities in government agencies.

344. <u>Agenda for Comparative Studies in Adult Education: Report</u>

<u>from the International Expert Meeting, 1972</u>.

Occasional Papers no. 29. Syracuse University,

Publications in Continuing Education, 1972. 77p.

Thirty-five of the leading figures in adult education
from fifteen countries report and analyze international
comparative studies of adult education. A full report
will soon be published.

345. Aker, George F. <u>Adult Education Procedures, Methods and</u>

<u>Techniques; A Classified and Annotated Bibliography</u>

<u>1953-1963</u>. Syracuse: Library of Continuing Education

at Syracuse University, 1965. 163p.

This bibliography has been compiled to systematize
and organize the expanding body of knowledge about procedures in adult education. The bibliography is classified
into the following categories: general references, residential centers for continuing education, individual and
group methods, and techniques of adult education.

346. American Institute of Certified Public Accountants.

<u>Professional Development 1971</u>. New York: American

Institute of Certified Public Accountants, 1971.

This institute plans in advance continuing education
programs for one year and prints these in a booklet for
all members. Basically, it plans six types of programs
using a wide assortment of educational methods: seminars,
courses, workshops, lecture programs, training programs,
individual study materials. State societies assume the
responsibility of offering the programs throughout the
nation.

347. Association of American Library Schools, Committee on

Continuing Library Education. <u>Mini-Workshop on</u>

<u>Continuing Education in Architecture, Engineering,</u>

<u>Education, Banking, and the Ministry Proceedings</u>.

Sponsored by the AALS Committee on Continuing Library

Education for the CLEN Network. Washington, D.C.,

January, 1973. 25p. (Mimeographed).

Presented are questions and answers concerning continuing education in five professions other than library science. The American Institute of Architects, for example, has two divisions for continuing education-- one deals with behavior, skills, and how to do things, the other is information. For the latter, a cassette called RAP, for "The Review of Architectural Periodicals" comes out once a month. The hour tape condenses and rank orders the items by priority of importance. Fifty journals and varied newsletters are searched. Another information source is also cassette based by subject and may include accompanying written matter. A third source of information is a computerized reference service system which lists all of the programs at universities and other associations that would be relevant to architects.

348. Barrett, Gerald V. and others. <u>Combating Obsolescence</u>

<u>Using Perceived Discrepancies in Job Expectations of</u>

<u>Research Managers and Scientists</u>. Rochester, New York:

University of Rochester, Management Research Center,

1970. 28p.

Research and development scientists, engineers, and managers completed a questionnaire covering their preferences and expectations about future conditions in their careers. Of the 143 respondents who answered the "Exercise Future" questionnaire, 75 percent considered educational updating desirable but only 44 percent expected to have time to take any courses to overcome obsolescence. Few respondents expected to achieve freedom from organizational constraints to choose new projects or set individual schedules.

349. Borg, Walter R. <u>The Minicourse: Rationale and Uses in the</u>

<u>Inservice Education of Teachers</u>. Washington, D.C.:

Office of Education, 1968. 28p. ED 024 647.

This collection of materials reports the research
and development of a series of in-service training short
courses (about seventy-five minutes per day for fifteen
days) designed to teach specific teacher behavior patterns
with use of the microteaching technique, self-evaluation
of video-tape feedback, instructional films, and filmed
illustrations by model teachers. The main document reviews
the instructional model, defines and discusses the advantages of microteaching, and describes the scope and
future plans for the minicrouse program.

350. Botzman, Harvey. <u>Resources for Continuing Nursing Educa-</u>

<u>tion in the Genesee Region, New York State</u>, 1973.

112p. ED 079 570.

A study was conducted to: 1) ascertain the nature
and extent of continuing education for nurses in the Genesee
region; 2) determine if an interest exists among health
care and educational agencies for a cooperative effort to
plan, develop, and produce continuing education activities for nurses; and 3) provide one data source for future
planning of such activities. A total of eight continuing
education resources were identified: agency information,
cooperation, educational activities, information dissemination, facilities, finance, personnel, and records.

351. Burgess, Paul. "Reasons for Adult Participation in Group

Educational Activities." <u>Adult Education</u>. 22 (No. 1)

3-29.

Additional information on why adults participate in educational activities appears to be necessary if the field of adult education is to continue to improve educational offerings. The results herein affirm the hypothesis that reasons chosen by men and women for participating in educational activities will factor into seven groups: the desire: 1) to know, 2) to reach a personal goal, 3) to reach a social goal, 4) to reach a religious goal, 5) to escape, 6) to take part in an activity, and 7) to comply with formal requirements.

352. California. University--Ad Hoc Faculty Planning Committee. Proposed Program of Mid-Career Education for Public Administrators in Metropolitan Areas. Prepared by Frederick C. Mosher. Berkeley: University of California, 1966.

This proposed program of continuing education for state and local officials involved in metropolitan affairs offers three types of programs of differing lengths. The program outlines are presented as well as a discussion of the basic considerations involved in the development of this plan. Appendices include suggested syllabi of courses and topics and excerpts from memoranda of committee members concerning the problem and the program.

353. Carlson, Robert A. Conceptual Learning: From Mollusks to Adult Education. Occasional Papers no. 35. Syracuse University. ERIC Clearinghouse on Adult Education, 1973. 33p.

This literature review proposes to offer the practitioner and student of adult education an overview of conceptual learning. Tracing the movement's intellectual and political growth, it lists recent seminal studies in the field and presents a series of relatively nontechnical

interpretations of them. It pinpoints the small amount
of literature thus far produced relating conceptual
learning directly to adult education. Perhaps, most
important of all, the review suggests a number of
philosophical implications behind conceptual learning.

354.   The Carnegie Commission on Higher Education. Less Time,

        More Options; Education Beyond the High School.

        New York: McGraw-Hill Book Company, 1971. 45p.

        This special report examines and makes recommenda-
tions concerning the general flow of students into and
through the formal structure of higher education in the
United States. Degrees play a key role in this flow.
Recommendations are set forth calling for basic changes
in the pattern of this flow. Nine major themes are
presented. Three relate specifically to continuing education: 1) opportunities for higher education and the
degrees it affords should be available to persons
throughout their lifetimes and not just immediately after
high school; 2) more educational, and thus career, opportunities should be available to all those who wish to
study part-time or return to study later in life; and
3) society would gain if work and study were mixed
throughout a lifetime, thus reducing the sense of
sharply compartmentalized roles of isolated students
vs. workers and of youth vs. older members of society.

355.   Charters, Alexander N. and Rivera, William M., eds.

        International Seminar on Publications in Continuing

        Education. Papers presented at Third International

        Seminar on Adult Education. Syracuse, New York:

        Syracuse University Press, 1972. 124p.

        The seminar focuses on publications in the profes-
sional field of adult education. Some of the papers
presented are: "Thoughts on Periodicals for Professionals"

by Thomas Kelley; "Use of Publications by Adult Education Scholars" by Allen B. Knox; and "Needs of the Users of Publications from the Practitioner's Point of View" by Olivia B. Stokes and Alice M. Leppert.

356. Chenevier, J. "La Révolution de L'Education Permanente."

Convergence. 3 (no. 4, 1970), 56-59.

The author, a French oil industrialist, is committed to continuing education and recommends four steps to improve it: 1) the student needs to learn how to learn and enjoy the process; 2) barriers between cultural and utilitarian education must be broken down; 3) a generalist education of adults is good background for readyness to learn specialized information; and 4) youth should spend fewer years in formal academic programs. Continuing education is a better means of providing training to youth than a university diploma as a guarantee of employment.

357. Cohen, David and Dubin, Samuel S. "A Systems Approach to

Updating Professional Personnel." In: National

Seminar on Adult Education Research. Toronto,

February 9-11, 1969. University Park, Pa.:

Pennsylvania State University, February, 1969. 12p.

ED 025 718.

Presented is a systems analysis model to assist both educators and professionals to keep up-to-date in their fields. The model includes psychological, motivational, and educational characteristics. Through the mathematical model, the most important variables can be delineated. However, the model does not provide for negative feedback and the problem of statistical estimation remains inconclusive.

358. <u>Continuing Education for R and D Careers: An Exploratory</u>

<u>Study of Employer-Sponsored and Self-Teaching Models</u>

<u>of Continuing Education in Large Industrial and</u>

<u>Federal Government Owned R & D Laboratories</u>. Pre-

pared for the National Science Foundation by Social

Research Inc., Chicago, 1969. 226p. ED 035 813.

Research and development scientists and engineers in
industry and the Federal government were questioned in
terms of their needs and use of continuing professional
education. Three approaches to continuing education were
found: 1) subsidized short-term courses; 2) professional
meetings, lectures, sabbaticals, and lectures; and
3) journal clubs and other in-house activities. Employer
programs consisted of various combinations of the above
three approaches. Scientists and engineers in university
settings gave more weight to research and degree teaching
than to continuing education. Recommendations are made
for improving continuing education opportunities for
management, universities, and professional societies.

359. <u>Continuing Education in the Professions</u>. Current Infor-

mation sources no. 24. Syracuse, New York: ERIC

Clearinghouse on Adult Education, Syracuse University,

1969. ED 033 250.

This is a 225-item, annotated bibliography on professional continuing education in ten areas including
library science.

360. <u>Continuing Education Programs in Nursing. Two Documents</u>:
     <u>The Florida Nurses Association Landmark Statement</u>
     <u>and Maryland Practical Nurses Association Continuing</u>
     <u>Education Program</u>. Orlando, Florida Nurses Associa-
     tion; Baltimore, Maryland Licensed Practical Nurses
     Association, 1973. 7p. ED 091 607.

   The Florida Nurses Association has set up standards
for continuing education certification. One reason for
granting certification is to encourage nurses to participate in continuing education programs. The standards
stipulate four basic points: certification, the manner
in which recognition is given, the planned use of the
continuing education unit (CEU), and the requirements
for certification. Professional participation and activities are considered in terms of the contact hours and
their applicability to the CEU. Outlined are procedures
for obtaining CEU for programs.

   The Maryland Licensed Practical Nurses Association
defines the nature of the continuing education program,
lists the objectives which the application of CEU will
fulfill, and stipulates the administration of the continuing education program. Steps for recording CEU are
itemized, and standards for determining credit are established.

361. <u>The Continuing Education Unit. State Plan for Educational</u>
     <u>Institutions of Higher Learning in Iowa</u>. Iowa State
     Coordinating Committee for Continuing Education.
     Des Moines. 1974. 39p. ED 089 141.

   The above state plan includes guidelines for inaugurat-
ing Continuing Education Unit (CEU) programs in Iowa. CEU
means at least ten contact hours of participation in a
structured continuing education experience. The sponsor

is required to have qualified instructors and a curriculum
with behavioral objectives and criteria. The guidelines
specify some of the mechanics to be followed in a CEU
program: registration, record forms, the layout of
keypunch cards, a program classification system, and
structured recordkeeping. The appendix includes samples
of the above forms, a planned CEU record system at the
University of Iowa, and a description of the CEU award
sequence. Academic and occupational areas are treated
separately with descriptions of codes, titles, and content.

362. <u>Continuing Engineering Studies--A Report of the Joint

Advisory Committee</u>. New York: Engineer's Council for

Professional Development, 1965.

The role of the Joint Committee is to study the overall situation in continuing engineering education, consider the respective roles of universities, societies,
industries, and government in continuing education, and
to make specific recommendations.

363. Corson, John J. and R. Shale Paul. <u>Men Near the Top:

Filling Key Posts in the Federal Service</u>. Baltimore,

Maryland: Johns Hopkins Press, 1966.

"The need is for the establishment of a career-long
process that will utilize all means to equip the individual with the variety of competencies required at the
top in the program field he has chosen." In regard to
university training, Corson warns that it can provide
stimulation for learning only if the university recognizes
the individual's own need and does not force the individual into rigid programs reflecting the faculty's
conception of the executive's needs, or into courses and
seminars designed for the training or Ph.D. candidates
in teaching and research.

364. Cory, N. Durward. <u>Incentives Used in Motivating Profes-</u>
     <u>sional Growth of Teachers</u>. Minneapolis: University
     of Minnesota, 1969. 23p. ED 027 254.

     This publication is the product of a project designed
     to study problems of in-service teacher education and to
     assemble data on promising practices that might stimulate
     schools to develop vigorous programs of professional
     growth. Included are lists of sixty practices principals
     have found to be effective and sixty incentives listed
     by teachers as the most promising in their own school
     systems.

365. Cummings, Roy J. "Removing Intuition from Course Develop-
     ment: Methods at FAA (Federal Aviation Administra-
     tion) to Prevent Overtraining and Undertraining."
     <u>Training and Development Journal</u>. 22 (January 1968),
     18-27.

     Industrial training courses are developed by engineers,
     scientific and research specialists, training directors,
     and others. While they are experts in their fields, they
     are not knowledgeable in the science of learning theory.
     As a partial remedy, the author describes the necessary
     steps course designers can take to implement an effective
     training course. The steps are to identify and record
     the job tasks, determine the performance requirements of
     the job, and appraise the qualifications possessed by the
     trainees. This information is used to formulate a train-
     ing requirement which in turn will lead course developers
     to design course and lesson outcomes.

366. Deinum, Andries. <u>Speaking for Myself; A Humanist Approach</u>
     <u>to Adult Education for a Technical Age</u>. Center for
     the Study of Liberal Education for Adults, Boston
     University, 1966. 94p.

This work includes notes and essays on education for adults. Topics covered are: university extension and program development, university and education television, and continuing higher education--an essay in quotations.

367. Delker, Paul V. "Governmental Roles in Lifelong Learning." Journal of Research and Development in Education.

32 (Summer 1974), 24-33.

Lifelong learning is broader than adult education, but adult education is an essential element in lifelong learning. There are four essential elements to a life-long learning system: 1) an effective core-education for all citizens; 2) multiple learning opportunities; 3) multiple education opportunities; and 4) equitable access to learning and education opportunities. The author, Director of the Division of Adult Education, U.S. Office of Education, gives the current administration view that government should have no role in providing services and effecting social systems if these can be achieved by non-governmental units. Also, nothing should be carried out by a higher, more centralized unit of government that can be effectively achieved by a lesser unit of government. Throughout the paper, the author stresses that governmental units involved in the implementation of the four elements of lifelong learning are principally the local and state units regulating education. In line with President Nixon's 1974 education message, the author states that "the greatest promise lies in placing the decision for determining what shall be learned, when, where and how in the hands of the learner." Theoretically, every citizen would have available a choice of grants, loans, sabbaticals, or combinations of these from which to choose.

368. Dellefield, Calvin. <u>Professional Development: A Priority</u>

   <u>of the National Advisory Council on Vocational Edu-</u>

   <u>cation</u>. Raleigh: North Carolina State University.

   Center for Occupational Education. 1974. 8p.

   ED 094 194.

   The National Advisory Council on Vocational Education
has as one of its goals for 1974-75, the implementation
of professional personnel development programs in career
and vocational education. Realistic experiences in the
use of recent teaching materials and methods are needed
in pre- and in-service programs of teacher training
institutes. The council committee makes several recommendations for changes in counseling and guidance. Career
education resources are listed as well as new appointees
in the Bureau of Occupational and Adult Education.

369. Dill, William R.; Crowston, Wallace B.S.; and Elton,

   Edwin J. "Strategies for Self-Education." <u>Harvard</u>

   <u>Business Review</u>. 43 (December 1965), 119-30.

   The threat of personal obsolescence is a challenge
at all levels. Management wants continuing education in
skills and knowledge to directly contribute to the organization through higher sales and/or increased efficiency.
For success with any of the strategies of self-education,
several general rules apply. The effort, whether it involves reading or reflecting on experience, should be
selective and focused, guided by an agenda on goals for
learning. A learner must be willing to admit that education consists not just in acquiring new knowledge,
skills, and attitudes, but also in giving up convictions
and approaches to problems that may be inaccurate and out-
moded. New knowledge, skills, and attitudes are secure
only when they have been integrated with those acquired
earlier.

370. Doherty, Victor W. "The Carnegie Professional Growth

Program: An Experiment on the In-Service Education

of Teachers." Journal of Teacher Education. 18

(Fall 1967), 261-68.

The Carnegie Professional Growth Program has resulted
in the development of over 140 courses and workshops for
teachers. Courses are closely tailored to the needs of
specific teacher groups. Main achievements include a
heightened interest in using objectives in instructional
planning, observable professional growth of participants,
and sharper focus on teacher needs.

371. Drucker, Peter F. and others. Oakland Papers: Symposium

on Social Change and Educational Continuity. Notes

and Essays on Education for Adults, 51. Brookline,

Mass.: Center for the Study of Liberal Education

for Adults. 1966. 80p. ED 030 044.

The Kellogg Foundation sponsored an alumni program
at Oakland University. The papers presented here discuss
continuing education opportunities for its graduates.
Peter Drucker expresses his views on "The University in
an Educated Society." Patterns of learning need to
evolve due to the pressures of a growing technical society.
Max Learner writes on "The University in an Age of Revo-
lutions." Rollo May discusses man's drive for an expanding consciousness and the needs resulting from this drive.
He concludes that education falls short of meeting these
needs. In "The University and Institutional Change,"
Margaret Mead argues that the traditional commitments
and dispositions of educational institutions handicap
them in adapting to change.

372. Dryer, Bernard V., ed. "Lifetime Learning for Physicians:

Principles, Practices, Proposals." Journal of Medical

Education. 37 (June 1962), 1-134.

This comprehensive "landmark" report emphasizes the
necessity for cooperative, long-range planning by all
concerned professional groups if lifetime professional
education is to be achieved within a profession. The
study has three major parts: 1) principles (based on
assumptions); 2) practices based on the criteria considered necessary for continuing education programs--
excellence of content, personal satisfaction, freedom of
choice, continuity, accessibility, and convenience; and
3) proposals for action. Eight health related national
professional associations sponsored and jointly developed
the study.

373. Dubin, Samuel S. "Obsolescence of Lifelong Education: A

Choice for the Professional." American Psychologist.

27 (May 1972), 486-98.

The author, a psychologist, argues that the rate of
change and the addition of new data and knowledge hasten
professional obsolescence. After defining the meaning of
obsolescence, he gives some of its symptoms and causes
and present efforts being made to cope with it. He
describes methods of providing motivation for professional
updating, measuring, and assessing professional competence.
He concludes that research in continuing education is
embarrassingly light, both in quantity and quality.

374. Dubin, Samuel S., Alderman, Everett and Marlow, LeRoy.

"Keeping Managers and Supervisors in Local Government

Up-to-Date." Public Administration Review. 29

(May-June 1969), 294-98.

Summarized are the major findings of a study by the Department of Planning Studies, Continuing Education, The Pennsylvania State University, entitled "Educational Needs of Managers and Supervisors in Cities, Boroughs, and Townships in Pennsylvania." Of the 138 managers who responded, over half of them indicated that they "should have" more course work in management development, public relations and public reporting, effective communication in the organization, and budget administration. Managers also indicated which subjects represented educational needs of those they supervised. Background information of the managers is summarized as well as any continuing education activities in which they have participated. Four aspects of updating considered were the attitude of the manager's superior toward education, municipal policy on professional development, in-service training, and financial assistance plans.

375. DuBois, Edward. "Case for Employee Education."

Management Bulletin, No. 160. New York: American

Management Association, 1967.

Employee education implies that the person is internally motivated to learn; he takes the initiative to learn. In employee training, the content is important to the employer but may appear as a tedious job requirement to the employee. The author refers to psychological theories that management can utilize in continuing education for employees in business. The complete case for employee education thus includes reasons of public policy, of community relations, and of payback.

376. Essert, Paul L. and Spence, Ralph B. "Continuous Learning

Through the Educative Community: An Exploration of

the Family-Educational, the Sequential Unit, and the

Complementary-Functional Systems." Adult Education

Journal. 28 (1968), 260-71.

The authors propose a definition of the educative
community and identify three major component systems:
the family system, the sequential unit system, which includes schools, colleges, and universities, and the
complementary-functional system, which provides sytematic
learning not learned or inadequately learned in the other
two systems. The paper analyzes the elements, resources,
and needs of the educative community, discusses the implications for program learning, and suggests some of the
responsibilities of adult educators to the three systems.

377. Feldman, Raymond, ed. Whither WICHE in Continuing

Psychiatric Education of Physicians; Training Institute

for Psychiatrist-Teachers of Practicing Physicians.

(10th Annual Meeting, Salt Lake City, Utah,

February 5-8, 1970). Boulder, Colorado: Western

Interstate Commission for Higher Education, 1970.

56p. ED 044 069.

Several papers on continuing psychiatric education
are presented in this report. Mr. Feldman examines the
role of WICHE past, present, and future. Other articles
are: "Use of the Physician Assistant" by Robert Senescu;
"Psychiatric Problems of Physicians in Rural Areas" by
John Waterman; "Long-Range Planning in Continuing Education" by Howard Kern; "Patient-Centered Teaching with
Video Tape" by Robert Daugherty; and "Teaching and Learning Techniques" by Carl Pollack.

378. Ferretti, Fred. "Educational Television." American

Libraries. 3 (April 1972), 366-84.

The growth of educational television is analyzed
from the 1950's to the enactment of the Public Broadcast-
ing Act in 1967 which changed educational TV to "public"

television. Congress legislated to it a broader scope
of the network concept. Educators see the medium as a
"soft sell." It should do more than broadcast courses
for credit; TV can hold people's attention, change
their views; people learn without being aware of learning.

Areas also discussed are public TV's treatment of
minorities, variance of coverage by local stations on
controversial topics; and the quality of documentary
reporting.

379. Fox, June I. "An Instructional Strategy for an Intensive

Short-Term Learning Environment." In: A Program

for Statewide Library Planning and Evaluation, 1971-

1973; An Evaluative Summary. Columbus, Ohio: Ohio

State University, 1973. pp. 1-26.

380. Frasure, Kenneth J. "Your Leadership Development Pro-

gram." Paper presented to the Annual Conference of

the American Association of School Administrators,

Atlantic City, New Jersey, February, 1968.

ED 021 330.

Various approaches to in-service education for administrators are discussed and specific recommendations
are made for improving programs of educational leadership
development.

381. Frenckner, T. Paulsson. "Development of Operational

Management Methods: What Does It Mean for the Edu-

cation of Managers?" International Social Science

Journal. 20 (no. 1, 1968), 28-34.

In regard to management education, it is necessary
to develop the following in management procedures: a
common operational language; a managerial discipline
based on the decision theory approach; a systems approach to the company, its environment and divisions.
The value of these procedures lies for the most part in
the development of a more efficient means of learning
from experience. Management is largely dependent upon
information derived from experiences and history because
outside forces affecting management can only be partially
predicted. Knowledge about the company and its environment should be emphasized in a management education program. It should include training in social adaptation,
economic judgment, technical skills, and especially,
the learning process itself.

382. Glancy, Keith E. and Rhodes, John A. Jr. The Continuing

Education Unit. Criteria and Guidelines. Final

Report of the National Task Force on the Continuing

Education Unit. Washington, D.C.: National Univer-

sity Extension Association. 1974. 42p.

"The Continuing Education Unit (CEU) has been
designed to facilitate the accumulation and exchange of
standardized information about individual participation
in non-credit continuing education." Content, format,
and methodology must first be ascertained to eliminate
preconceived ideas of program length, approaches, or
formats in implementing educational objectives. CEU
requires at least ten contact hours of participation in

a structured setting under the guidance of qualified instructors and sponsorship. CEU is applicable to education
administration, professional groups, and the individual.
Task Force guidelines list the appropriate use of CEU
and program criteria. The National Planning Conference
on the Feasibility of a Uniform Crediting and Certification System for Continuing Education conceived and funded
the project carried out by the Task Force.

383. Glass, J. Conrad Jr. "The Professional Churchman and

Continuing Education." Adult Leadership. 20 (April

1972), 349-50.

There are two broad areas which lend themselves to
the professional development of churchmen. To continually
update churchmen within the disciplines of the church, the
agencies best equipped to provide this type of training
are the schools of religious education and seminaries,
and the denominational boards and agencies. The second
area is the broad field of study of the behavioral
sciences. Churchmen need to know some of the key concepts political scientists are advocating in organization
and administration and what the best thinkers and re-
searchers in the field have to say about planning for
social change.

384. Haire, Mason. "Managing Management Manpower: A Model

for Human Resource Development." Business Horizons.

10 (Winter 1967), 23-28.

While business often plans for capital expansion,
product diversification, and increased market penetration,
seldom does it plan for providing the increased managerial
talent that the new ideas and future growth call for.
Described is a system for manpower management that includes training for new job levels and evaluation of individual performance.

385. Herzberg, Frederick. "Job Enrichment Pays Off." _Harvard Business Review_. 47 (March-April 1969), 49-67.

This article reports on five job enrichment studies which have been carried out in Imperial Chemical Industries, Ltd. and other British companies. The purpose of the studies was to shed light on important job enrichment questions dealing with the generality of the findings, the feasibility of making changes, and the consequences to be expected. In addition, the studies set out to determine how the concept of job enrichment may be most effectively applied in furthering the attainment of companies' business objectives.

386. Herzberg, Frederick. "One More Time: How Do You Motivate Employees?" _Harvard Business Review_. 46 (January, February 1968), 53-62.

The psychology of motivating employees is complex. Externally imposed attempts by management to motivate employees have met with failure. The absence of good supervisor-employee relations and liberal fringe benefits may make the employee unhappy, but their presence will not make him want to work harder. Other myths about motivation are reduction of time spent at work, human relations and sensitivity training, job participation, job counseling, and two-way communication. The only successful way to motivate the employee is to give him challenging work in which he can assume responsibility.

An experiment is described of vertical vs. horizontal job loading. The former provides motivator factors, the latter reduces the employee's personal contribution rather than giving him an opportunity for growth in his accustomed job. Those who have vertical job loading perform better and are more satisfied in their work. Ten steps are suggested to insure job enrichment. The changes should make the job challenging enough for the skills of the individual. Those who have more ability will be able to demonstrate it and be promoted to higher level jobs. Motivators have a longer-term effect on employee's attitudes than external incentives of salary and benefits.

387. Heyman, Margaret M. <u>Criteria and Guidelines for the Evalu</u>

<u>tion of In-service Training</u>. Department of Health,

Education and Welfare, Washington, D.C.: Social and

Rehabilitation Service, 1968. 35p.

Criteria and guidelines are suggested for evaluating
the adequacy and effectiveness of in-service training
programs for use in administrative review of staff
development in state and local departments of public
welfare. The content of orientation and training is
touched upon, together with administrative and learning
factors in the choice of training methods. Structural
factors, type of change and learning, criteria from
curriculum planning theory are also discussed.

388. Honey, John C. "A Report: Higher Education for Public

Service." <u>Public Administration Review</u>. 27

(November 1967), 294-321.

In this report, higher education refers to all study
beyond high school. For universities public service
means service to the community as a companion function
to research and teaching. Some universities will need
to play a new role in establishing programs of public
administration and public affairs to stimulate public
service. Today, public administration concerns itself
with a broader scope beyond budgeting, personnel, and
organization and management problems. This report equates
public administration with the total governmental process
(executive, legislative, and judicial), in both its
career and political aspects. Discussed in this report
are the professions and professional education in relation to public service. Nine proposals for immediate
action are recommended.

389. Horn, Francis H. Tomorrow's Targets for University Adult

Education. Tenth Annual Seminar on Leadership in

University Adult Education. Michigan State Univer-

sity, Continuing Education Service. 1967. ED 019 536.

Scientific and technological advances, the population
explosion, increasing leisure, rising educational levels
and expectations, and the growing complexity of public
issues have direct implications for university adult
education. Although the adult educational role of liberal
arts colleges and junior colleges will and must continue
to increase, universities must provide leadership in this
area because they alone are committed to the improvement
of society in all its aspects and have the research
personnel to contribute significantly to the task. Objectives must include not only doctoral and post-doctoral
work and professional continuing education but also the
expansion of liberal arts education in both the sciences
and the humanities, and provisions for groups (notably
women and retired persons) who have not been part of the
regular clientele of university adult programs.

390. Hospital Continuing Education Project. Training and

Continuing Education: A Handbook for Health

Care Institutions. Chicago: Hospital Research

and Education Trust, 1970.

This book describes techniques used in the development of continuing education programs. The objective is
to improve and expand educational opportunities for
hospital personnel through cooperation between hospital
associations and universities.

391. Houle, Cyril O. "The Comparative Study of Continuing Pro-

fessional Education." Convergence. 3 (no. 4, 1970),

3-12.

Professor Houle notes that while many professions have continuing education programs regarding their own principles and practices, they have not made the effort to compare the methods employed by each profession to accomplish this common task. The author examines the value of comparative analysis as applied to continuing professional education. One topic for comparative study would be the analysis of learning processes and procedures. Four possible approaches are outlined. Another topic for comparative study deals with problems common to all professions. Although the above two topics have immediate usefulness in practice, continuing education needs to be grounded in theoretical foundations and a clear understanding of the nature of a profession. The term "profession" is analyzed; thirteen aims of any group that calls itself a profession are given. Professionalization is based on discovery, growth, and innovation whether the individual is in an entrepreneurial, collective, or hierarchical occupation.

392. Houle, Cyril O. "The Role of Continuing Education in

Current Professional Development." ALA Bulletin.

61 (March 1967), 259-67.

The concept of professionalism can only survive if there is continuing education. The beginning professional cannot possibly take all the courses necessary to include all he needs to know. Some of what he has been taught may not be true or discarded as meaningless as new knowledge evolves. It is assumed that the young professional has an inquiring mind and will make the effort to keep abreast of new knowledge in his profession; will continue his study of the basic disciplines which support his profession; and will grow as a person as well as a professional. Ultimately the individual is himself responsible for his own education while the professional association bears the chief collective responsibility for it.

393. Houle, Cyril O. "To Learn the Future." <u>Medical Clinics</u>

of North America. 54 (January 1970), 6-7.

Emphasizing the concept of interprofessional cooperation, Dr. Houle recommends that members of each profession
should not act as though they alone had any need of continuing study and should drop the assumption that their
processes are wholly unique.

394. "The Individual Education Unit and Its Place in Con-

tinuing Education." <u>Cadence</u>. Special Continuing

Education Issue. 4 (November-December 1973), 1-70.

The seven articles in this issue answer many questions regarding the Continuing Education Unit (CEU) for
professional continuing education. The writers document
the relevance of CEU and its current applications in the
professions. Another unit discussed is the Individual
Education Unit (IEU) which recognizes one hour of participation in a continuing education learning experience
(the CEU requires ten hours of preparation). Another new
program is Professional Acknowledgement for Continuing
Education (PACE). The IEU and the CEU have been used in
the field of medical technology.

IEU, PACE, and CEU are discussed in the following
articles: "Professional Societies and Continuing Educa-
tion" by David Lindberg, "PACE" by Gregory C. Roach,
"Continuing Education; National Observations" by Fred
Struve, "Why Equivalency? For Whom? and How?" by Thelma
Golden, "Social Factors Influencing Medical Technology
Education" by Willa Hedrick, and "Continuing Education--
Why Is It Necessary?" by Annamarie Barios.

395. <u>Investment for Tomorrow; A Report of the Presidential</u>

<u>Task Force on Career Advancement</u>. Washington, D.C.:

Civil Service Commission, 1967. 75p. ED 041 199.

The Presidential Task Force on Career Advancement
reviewed post-entry training for federal employees in
professional, administrative, and technical occupations.
Some agency training does not provide knowledge or develop
skills needed by management before they are advanced to
higher levels. Agencies differ widely in the extent and
quality of training for specialists. The absence of
development programs with the resultant loss of peak performance can cost more than training.

396. Jessup, F. W., ed. Lifelong Learning; A Symposium on

Continuing Education. Headington Hill Hall, Oxford,

England: Pergamon Press, 1969. 178p. ED 029 270.

Consideration is given to the idea of lifelong learning and its implications for British institutions of
formal education, professional continuing education in
the United States and Britain, educational activities
of voluntary associations, the education responsibility
of the public authorities, and educational expenditures
as a reflection of social and economic policy.

397. Johnstone, John W. C. Volunteers for Learning; A Study

of the Educational Pursuits of American Adults.

Chicago: Aldine Publishing Company, 1965.

The National Opinion Research Center made a survey
of the nature of adult education in the United States.
The inquiry focused on the educational experiences of
Americans following termination of regular full-time
school attendance. The inquiry had four phases: 1) to
provide a general description of the scope and nature of
adult participation in formal and informal educational
endeavors of all kinds; 2) to examine the social and
psychological factors which influence educational behavio
3) to examine the factors in phase 2 with attention focuse
on people between the ages of seventeen and twenty-four;

and 4) to determine the nature of facilities for adult
education in "typical" urban centers to gain a better
understanding of the variety of educational programs
currently available to adults and the level of awareness
and use of these facilities. The methodology and findings of the study are detailed in this report.

398. Kemp, Florence B. Noncredit Activities in Institutions

   of Higher Education, 1967-68 Institutional Distri-

   bution. Washington, D.C.: U.S. Government Printing

   Office, 1970. 25p.

   One-half of the institutions of higher education in
the United States offered non-credit continuing education activities in 1967-68. While the traditional methods
of instruction retain importance in terms of number of
institutions using them, the widespread use of the conference, institute and workshop methods stands out
accounting for about 46 percent of the non-credit
registrations.

399. Kidd, J. Roby, ed. Convergence. 3(no. 4, 1970), 94p.

   The entire issue of this international journal of
adult education is devoted to continuing professional
education. The articles are in several languages.
J. Chenevier writes of "La Revolution de L'Education
Permanente"; Zoya Malkora discusses in English "Research
in Comparative Education at the U.S.S.R. Academy of
Educational Sciences." Leonid Zeidlits notes trends in
"The Professional Growth of Physicians in the Soviet
Union"; Derek J. Buchanan denotes changes in "Professional
Attitudes to Continuing Education in England." Korlheinz
Rebel of West Germany writes on "The Necessity of Further
Education in the Professions and Home Study as a Means
of Realization." Following each article is an abstract
in English, Spanish, French, and Russian.

400. Kimberly-Clark Corporation. Research and Engineering.

"Bank-Account." Policy for Continuing Education:

Environment for Growth. Neenah, Wisconsin:

Kimberly-Clark, 1968.

This is an example of an industry which believes in
the capacity and growth potential of the individual. It
offers a concrete systemized plan for providing time and
money allowances for continuing education in the form of
updating and refresher study and graduate and postgraduate
fellowships.

401. Knezevich, Stephen J. The Development and Testing of a

Model for a Nationally Based Vehicle Dedicated to

the Continuing Professional Growth of School Ad-

ministrators. Final Report. Washington, D.C.:

American Association of School Administrators, 1969.

137p. ED 030 194.

The primary objectives of the study were to develop
a model for a National Academy for School Executives, to
determine the receptivity of school administrators to such
a program, and to determine the feasibility of implementing the model within the near future. It was decided that
it is fiscally feasible to launch the short-term seminars
and clinics but more development is needed on the other
levels; the probability of attendance by administrators
at short-term programs is primarily related to the program
content, length of the program, and the fee charged.

402. Knowles, Malcolm S. <u>The Modern Practice of Adult Educa-</u>

   <u>tion: Andragogy Versus Pedagogy</u>. New York:

   Association Press, 1970. 384p.

   The author coins a new term to describe adult educa-
tion--andragogy. Pedagogy refers to the education of a
child; andragogy refers to the technology of educating
an adult. This book serves as a guide in planning and
as a reference for solving problems in informal adult
education. It deals with the emerging role of the adult
educator, emerging technology for adult learning, means
of establishing an organizational structure and climate,
assessing needs and interests in program planning,
defining purposes and objectives; designing, operating,
and evaluating comprehensive programs; and tools for
planning.

403. Knox, Alan B. <u>Continuing Professional Education</u>. 1972.

   15p.

   This paper is presented as part of a course at the
University of Illinois on continuing education. This
general article covers many aspects of the topic--the
need, scope, settings, planning, and conducting continuing
education for professionals.

404. Knox, Alan B. "Extension Education." <u>Encyclopedia of</u>

   <u>Educational Research</u>. 4th ed. New York: Macmillan.

   1969. p. 481-87.

   Extension education refers to any on-going, systematic program for adult part-time learners offered by
higher education institutions. Various types of continuing higher education programs are described. An
organization analysis of continuing higher education
divisions is given. The four major sections of this
article address the following areas: 1) the establishment and evaluation of outcomes; 2) the acquisition of
needed inputs; 3) the steps of changing inputs into

outcomes; and 4) trends in continuing higher education.
Each section includes an overview of research on continuing higher education as well as specific references
to research on university extension, Cooperative Extension Service, and college extension. The article's primary
focus concerns analysis of educational activities in which
students devote several sessions to the systematic study
of a subject.

405. Knox, Alan B. "Higher Education and Lifelong Learning."

Journal of Research and Development in Education.

7 (Summer 1974), 13-23.

This article deals with the relationship between institutions of higher education and adults involved in
lifelong learning. It focuses on two fictitious examples
of an administrator and a school teacher as participants
in continuing education activities, working through universities as sponsoring institutions. The junior college
administrator defines the group he wants to reach (under-
educated adults); lists the problem on which he wants to
focus (increase attendance in community problem courses);
gathers other data on sociology of the clientele (how to
market the courses, etc.); gets other professional
opinions; specifies alternative solutions to the problem;
develops a plan of action; and lists criteria to determine success or failure of the program. A university
professor works with the administrator through each step
of the process. This continuing education program links
up the knowledge and resources of the university community
with the everyday implementation problems of the "real
world."

406. Kreitlow, Burton W. Educating the Adult Educator. Part I

Concepts for the Curriculum. Madison, Wisconsin:

Experimental Station, College of Agriculture, Uni-

versity of Wisconsin, 1965. 25p. ED 023 969.

This is the first of a two-part research and development study on the education of adult educators. Part I is concerned with the relationship of adult education to selected fields of study. Information was gathered by comparing recent adult education research with that given in earlier reviews, going over research in other areas, and interviewing 34 selected leaders in these areas. The disciplines of psychology and sociology were particularly helpful in such areas as adoption, aging, leisure, social class, adult learning and characteristics, motivation, educational methods, and educational leadership. Of less impact, but of some value, were contributions from economics, communications, anthropology, public school and higher education, social work, school administration, vocational and military training, and library science.

407. Kreitlow, Burton W. Educating the Adult Educator. Part II:

Taxonomy of Needed Research. Report from the Adult

Re-Education Project. Madison, Wisconsin: Research

Development Center for Cognitive Learning, University

of Wisconsin, 1968. 27p. ED 023 031.

This theoretical report is the second of a two-part examination of the issue of the education of adult educators. Part I deals with the relationship of adult education to other disciplines. Part II sets up a design for categorizing areas of needed research in the area of adult education. This design is based on application--learning, teaching, guidance, and other activities. Three interrelated categories of application are used: 1) the adult as individual and learner, 2) the adult's response to social and cultural change, and 3) the adult education enterprise.

408. Lazarus, Charles Y. "Quest for Excellence--A Businessman's

Responsibility." Bulletin of Business Research. 43

(May 1968), 1+

The author, a businessman and former President of
the American Retail Federation, argues that the urban
crisis of crime and riots is a very real problem that
no single group or agency can solve. Educational institutions are producing better educated, better trained
graduates in the traditional skills of management but are
almost totally insensitive in eduacting them to the need
for understanding of community affairs and deep, personal
involvement. To verify this observation, the author
cites the conclusions of a survey of business school
graduates. The results show that middle management
employees do what they think the boss wants done; most
big business enterprises are ignoring problems on the
community front; and community activity has received
little emphasis in business school curriculums. The
last point is also true of undergraduate training.

409. Liveright, A. A. "Learning Never Ends: A Plan for Con-

tinuing Education." In: Alvin C. Eurich. Campus

1980; The Shape of the Future in American Higher

Education. New York: Delacorte Press, 1968. p. 149

The author depicts a mythical situation of a College
of Continuing Education at Metropolis University in 1980.
Although not yet a reality, component parts for such a
college already exist as programs in operation or on the
drawing board. The Appendix documents examples of these
programs.

The College of Continuing Education at Metropolis
U. has four institutes: 1) Occupational and Professional
Development, 2) Personal and Family Development, 3) Civic
and Social Development, and 4) Humanistic and Liberal
Development. As one of its functions, the Institute for
Occupational and Professional Development cooperates with
professional associations to set up and house (at its
inner city campus) a wide range of seminars and conferences to keep various professionals abreast of new findings in their fields. The college provides the faculty
either from Metropolis U. or other institutions while
the professional associations provide the technological
and operational information, and recruitment of students.

Other topics covered for establishing a College of Continuing Education are financing, administration and organization, accessibility to adults, community cooperation, and use of new educational technology.

410. Liveright, A. A., and Goldman, Freda H. <u>Significant</u>

<u>Developments in Continuing Higher Education.</u>

Occasional Paper, no. 12. Boston University, Center

for the Study of Liberal Education for Adults, 1965.

28p.

Higher adult education is today (1965) in a period of rapid and significant growth. There is a consequent need for new kinds of programs to develop professional personnel and to assist educators in more effective program planning. This article looks at the present status of adult education and identifies some significant developments that have occurred, and the future possibilities they point to.

411. Lloyd, Arthur P. <u>A Pilot Study Concerning the Continuing</u>

<u>Education Needs of the State of Idaho--Including a</u>

<u>Survey of the Continuing Education Needs of Idaho's</u>

<u>Classroom Teachers</u>. Boise: Idaho State Department

of Education, 1968. 58p. ED 083 204.

The report makes the assumption that education is not just for students or scholars but should fulfill the need for an "enlightened electorate." "Continuing education" is defined as including all forms of supplementary education provided through the efforts of numerous institutions and agencies from "cradle to grave." Idaho continuing education focuses on adult education that is not already a part of the function of educational institutions or agencies.

412. Long, Huey B. "Lifelong Learning: Pressures for Accept-

 ance." Journal of Research and Development in Edu-

 cation. 7 (Summer 1974), 2-12.

   With the rate of change in society and the rapid increase of knowledge, adult education is becoming a process
of lifelong learning. Three major pressures are con-
tributing to a public awareness of education beyond high
school and college. The first element is the human need
to adjust to change--to seek self-actualization. The
second element is the necessity of the individual to keep
pace with social and technological development. Adult edu
cation is the fastest growing sector in American education
In 1966, business and industry spent seventeen billion
dollars annually on education. The third source of
pressure is institutional. These institutional pressures
are of two kinds--philosophical and practical. The former
springs from the institutionalization of American education as the equalizer for opportunity in the economic
market place and the role of government in providing
educational access to all. The latter is institutionalize
self-interest. With decreased birth rates educational institutions have an oversupply of clients-students. The
author sees evidence of such institutionalized self-
interest in the recent widespread interest in non-
traditional higher education and the emergence of the
"continuing education unit."

   The writer makes a distinction between the concepts
of learning, education, and schooling. The purpose of
education should not be to transmit the culture or to
prepare the learner for a static society but it must
emphasize the learning to learn concept. By helping the
student learn how to learn, the learner becomes independen
of the teacher.

413. Luke, Robert A. The Role of the Professional Association

 in Continuing Professional Education. 1972. 15p.

   ED 069 946.

Presented is a discussion of those programs and activities of institutions of higher education, of employers and of professional associations which involve some sort of joint action on the part of any combination of two or more of any of the three groups. The focus of this discussion is on those training programs which require released time, depend upon cooperative decision making patterns, and are clearly aimed at systematic career development. The three major forces--the university, the professional association, and the employer-- are frequently completely separate and unrelated to each other. Brief description is given of the Adult Basic Education Professional Staff Development Program in the southeastern states.

414. Lynch, Patrick D., ed. and Blackstone, Peggy L., ed.

Institutional Roles for In-Service Education of

School Administrators. Albuquerque: New Mexico

University, 1966. 146p. ED 027 597.

This document is a compilation of papers read at a four-day conference attended by sixty participants throughout the U.S. Chapters include: "In-service Education of School Administrators: Background, Present Status and Problems," by Robert B. Howsam; "Psychological Processes in Influencing Change," by Stanley W. Caplan; and "The Development and Implementation of a Residence Executive Development Training Program."

415. Lynton, Rolf P. and Pareek, Udai. Training for Development.

Homewood, Illinois: Dorsey Press, 1967. 408p.

This book is concerned with training people on jobs in organizations. Training has three major phases: pre-training, training, and post-training. Each phase is discussed in detail. The trainer's attitudes and activities are examined in relation to the social processes

that help or hinder learning. The trainer's personality
is an important factor in choosing training methods and
activities. The authors include many examples of their
own experiences as trainers in various industrial and
community organizations. They summarize research findings and list additional readings.

416. Markel, J. Louise. "Training the New Employee." Science-

Technology News. 21 (Summer 1967), 34-35+.

Markel discusses the initial period of adjustment
and training of the new employee and stresses the necessity for the supervisor to allow for errors and confusion.
Several suggestions for facilitating the adjustment of
the new employee are offered.

417. McKeachie, Wilbert N. The Learning Process as Applied to

Short-Term Learning Situations. Preconference Work-

shop, Conference Proceedings, West Lafayette,

Indiana: Purdue University, National Extension

Association, Conference and Institute Division,

April 1965. 187p. ED 019 532.

This conference studies questions related to learning problems to be considered in planning and conferences
and institutes. Three major principles are: 1) learning
is always going on, so the problem is to plan what kinds
of learning will occur; 2) different kinds of learning
do not always go together, so choices must be made weighed
against what is foreclosed; and 3) feedback facilitates
learning.

418. McLeish, John A. B. "Continuing Professional Education

in Canada." Convergence. 3 (no. 4, 1970), 76-83.

Innovation and experimentation in continuing professional education are recent to Canada. Other than the problems of geography, scarcity of population, time and money, which inhibit continuing education, Canadian professional schools are conservative in their educational approach. Continuing professional education faces many of the same problems as other western countries--a steady growth toward group practice in the entrepreneurial profession, a decline in the number of generalists, and an increase in the number of interprofessional projects such as health science centers and community teams. The author cites some promising experiments underway in a number of professional fields in Canada. Three of the major religious denominations in Canada are implementing extended in-residence renewal programs for field clergy. Generally, the outlook for continuing education is bleak. Professional faculties fail to use the problem-solving approach in becoming involved in on-going projects. This problem is particularly acute among physicians who have a very low rate of participation in continuing education. Of promise for the seventies is the Professional Education Project which initiates new directions in professional education, especially through interprofessional exchange and dialogue. Professional faculties have joint meetings to discuss mutual problems and possible solutions.

419. McMahon, Ernest E.; Coates, Robert H.; and Knox, Alan B.

"Common Concerns: The Position of the Adult Education Association of the U.S.A." Adult Education Journal. 18 (Spring 1968), 192-213.

Fifteen interrelated concerns of adult education are identified. They are: 1) agencies of adult education, 2) adult education and the process of continuing change, 3) the American adult as a learner, 4) objectives of adult education programs, 5) learning experiences especially for adults, 6) evaluation to improve program effectiveness, 7) public understanding of adult education, 8) professionalization and staff development, 9) appropriate

facilities, 10) relations among adult education agencies,
11) relations with other agencies, 12) financing adult
education, 13) a body of professional knowledge, 14) research, and 15) international adult education. For each
concern a statement of the present situation, a list of
goals and a platform statement of the AEA of the U.S.A.
is given.

420. Meaney, John W., ed. and Carpenter, C. Ray, ed. Tele-

communications: Toward National Policies for Educa-

tion. The Report of the National Conference on Tele-

communications Policy in Education, The Georgia

Center for Continuing Education, Athens, Georgia,

December 4-6, 1968. Washington, D.C.: Joint Council

on Educational Telecommunication, 1970. 201p.

ED 044 917.

This report includes papers from a conference on telecommunications as well as discussion and recommendations
of the five conference commissions. Topics covered are
future information systems, cable television, satellite
systems, education and telecommunication, and others.
Telecommunications are applicable at every stage of the
education process--from preschool through the university
level and, ultimately, for continuing education.

The Joint Council on Educational Telecommunication
(JCET) makes several recommendations. Education and technology have an interrelated role to play in the near
future; cable TV will play a vital role in continuing education; and, programs are needed for training teachers in
the use and applications of telecommunications.

421. Miller, Harry L. <u>Teaching and Learning in Adult Education</u>.

New York: Macmillan Co., 1964. 340p.

This book is addressed to teachers and lay leaders
as well as to administrators. Each of the chapters on
small and large-group formats is a self-contained unit.
The text concentrates on the most widely useful core of
methodological principles and does not pretend to be
comprehensive.

422. Mosher, Frederick C. <u>Professional Education and the Public</u>

<u>Service; An Exploratory Study. Final Report</u>.

Berkeley: University of California, 1968. 170p.

ED 025 220.

The fastest growing occupational sectors in the U.S.
are the technical and professional fields. Government
employs at least one-third of all technical and professional workers especially in administrative positions
where greater influence can be exercised on public policy.
However, these two groups view themselves as members of
their respective academic disciplines rather than primarily
as public administrators. As a result, the field of public
administration has had less influence on public policy than
have other fields, possibly because it is not a specialized profession. There is no consensus on what constitutes
its core knowledge or what its skills and orientation
should be. Since most administrative positions are held
by subject specialists, students have little incentive to
pursue study in the field. Administration courses in
universities are usually based on organizational theories
of private business models rather than on the problems of
government administration. Hence, many professional administrators are not equipped with the skills, knowledge,
and attitudes to deal effectively with changing social
problems. To meet the problem, a research proposal is
presented to evaluate the roles of educational institutions
and governmental institutions and to determine what action
should be taken on their part to train public administrators.

423. Mulligan, Kathryn L. <u>A Question of Opportunity: Women</u>

     <u>and Continuing Education</u>. Washington, D.C.:

     National Advisory Council on Extension and Con-

     tinuing Education, 1973. 33p. ED 081 323.

        This document examines the role of women in con-
tinuing education. Part One reviews the relevant research concerning employment, traditional university
offerings, and vocational and educational lifestyles of
women. The results of a questionnaire sent to 376 program directors are described in Part Two in an attempt
to learn priorities for federal funds along with some of
the more successful models of programs for women.

424. National Institute of Mental Health. <u>An Annotated Bib-</u>

     <u>liography on In-Service Training for Allied Pro-</u>

     <u>fessionals and Non-professionals in Community Mental</u>

     <u>Health</u>. 1968. 64p.

        Materials citing experiences of formal community
health centers are included in this bibliography. Also
included are references on in-service mental health
training for professionals and non-professionals who
work in facilities other than mental health centers.

425. National Institute of Mental Health. <u>Annotated Bibliograph</u>

     <u>on In-Service Training in Mental Health for Staff in</u>

     <u>Residential Institutions</u>. 1968. 46p. ED 023 990.

        This annotated bibliography of periodical literature
through August of 1967 pertains to in-service mental
health training for personnel in residential institutions.
It includes materials on training in mental hospitals,
institutions for the mentally retarded, child care institutions, and nursing homes.

426. Nattress, Le Roy William, Jr. <u>Continuing Education for</u>

<u>the Professions</u>. Chicago: Natresources, Inc., 1970.

151p.

Fifteen articles cover the dimensions of continuing
professional education, the involvement of associations,
universities, and government. A model for continuing
professional education as well as clinical criteria of
instructional effectiveness are also included.

427. Nattress, Le Roy William, Jr. "Continuing Education for

the Professions in the United States." <u>Convergence</u>.

3 (no. 4, 1970), 42-50.

The author discusses the nature of a "profession"
and what constitutes "continuing education." A profession
is characterized as intellectual, learned, practical,
technical, organized, and altruistic. Continuing education is goal directed rather than activity oriented with
objectives stated in behavioral terms. It is a process
in which a person who has finished his formal education
is given a means for meeting needs for further professional development. Listed are several continuing professional education programs in the United States. For
example, continuing legal education is heavily content
and activity oriented. Continuing medical education has
received substantial Federal funding; there has been more
innovation in terms of techniques and methods than in
many other professional fields. Some of the innovations
include slow scan television programs, educational television dial access library, telephone and radio conferences, and others.

428. Nicholas, Robert A. <u>A Study of Continuing Education Needs</u>

<u>of Selected Professional Groups and University Exten-</u>

<u>sion Contract Programs in Wyoming</u>. Laramie: Univer-

sity of Wyoming, 1966. 207p.

This doctoral thesis presents a theory for a model
program of continuing professional education for faculty
at the University of Wyoming. First, there is a literature
review of the growth of the professions and the emergence
of continuing education. Special emphasis is given to
dentistry, medicine, law, architecture, and pharmacy.
Presented are 72 propositions concerning the organization
and administration of continuing education programs which
are rated by 39 leaders in the professions and 48 administrators of university programs. The results of the
responses are in several categories--administration,
extension guidelines, professional responsibility,
curriculum credits, evaluation, staffing and finance,
and others.

429. Niemi, John A. "Technology and Media for Lifelong Learn-

ing." Journal of Research and Development in Educa-

tion. 7 (Summer 1974), 77-86.

Technology and media have an important role to play
in relation to the concept of lifelong learning. Radical
approaches have been suggested to alter schools, colleges,
and universities away from their traditional roles of
terminal education. Technology and media can be applied
to expand and develop alternative systems in order to
serve large segments of the population. Learning by design
as opposed to learning by chance implies that the poten-
tialities of different media for instruction should relate
to the kind of learning outcomes that are desired. For
example, television and books are best suited to dispensing
information. As for the computer, it has the advantage
of providing feedback to the learner on his performance.
The author cites some examples of the variety of media
and technology which have been utilized in the individual
methods of correspondence study and programmed instruction.
The approaches used in reaching individuals can also be
extended to groups. Many attempts have been made to use
the mass media for educational purposes in North America.
The author lists some of the successes and failures.

430. Nyquist, Ewald B. "Planning for Continuing Education in
the 70's." Speech presented at the New York Association for Continuing Education Annual Meeting,
New York, May 18, 1971. 20p. ED 086 876.

In the 70's, four technologies (management technology,
cybernation, social engineering, and biological engineering) will produce vast changes, making demands upon continuous education as the greatest single resource for
meeting the challenge. Education may be expected to
become a social condition while the system of education
will be more flexible and open with increased opportunity
for adults. As a group, adult educators possess characteristics and virtues enabling them to adapt to change
and to accomplish goals in unfavorable climates. The
role of continuing education director encompasses ever
widening areas of knowledge and expertise. Among the
goals envisioned are a regionalization of continuing education services and a statewide planning system in New York.

431. O'Donnell, Cyril J. "Managerial Training: A System
Approach." Training and Development Journal.
22 (January 1968), 2-11.

The purpose of organized enterprise is to accomplish
objectives. To achieve these objectives, each enterprise
selects a manager who sets up a formal organization. The
ultimate objective is divided into specialties to work
toward that objective. The premise of this article is
that indifferent results in management training can be
attributed to obscurity of the objective--the purpose of
the training. The management process is explained as a
system in which a distinction is made between ends and means.
Training for the improvement of specific skills is not an
end in itself but is a means of aiding the manager to

achieve the objectives for which he is held accountable.
The source used for this purpose is training in managerial
appraisal. Discussed are management by results, discovery
of goals, relation of goals to end products, diagnosis of
performance, and corrective action that can be taken.

432. Ohliger, John. The Mass Media in Adult Education: A

Review of Recent Literature. Occasional Paper no. 18,

Syracuse University, ERIC Clearinghouse on Adult

Education, 1968. 123p.

This occasional paper surveys recent writing on the
use of communication and print media in adult education.
Included is an annotated bibliography. A section is
devoted to continuing professional education.

433. Osinski, Franklin W.; Ohliger, John and McCarthy, Colleen.

Toward Gog and Magog or?: A Critical Review of the

Literature of Adult Group Discussion. Occasional

Papers no. 30, Syracuse University, ERIC Clearing-

house on Adult Education, 1972. 82p.

A review is made of research on group discussion as
used in adult education within the context of the nature
of man and in relation to his ultimate end of self-
realization. It considers factors involved in group
discussion; its broad purposes, such as mutual education,
self-concept, and attitudes and interpersonal change;
and approaches to it--the role of leadership, non-
manipulative approaches, and human relations and sensitivity training. It then examines discussion in the
service of institutions--parent education, religious education for aging, and public affairs discussion. It reviews discussion and the mass media--international uses,
community education, and a recent scientific approach.

434. Proceedings of the Annual Seminar on Leadership in Con-

   tinuing Education. 11th Kellogg Center for Continuing

   Education, Michigan State University, April 8-11,

   1968. 55p. ED 021 192.

   The proceedings underline the conviction that the
final decades of the 20th century will make almost im-
possible demands on the wisdom, skill, and vision of
educators and leaders in continuing education. Seminar
papers discuss potential socioeconomic trends and influences in America, the problem of assessing the basic
nature of contemporary change, and the issues of in-
equality, the nature of education, the role of university
extension, and others.

435. Report; Professional Development Committee, National

   Association for Public School Adult Education.

   Washington, D.C.: National Association for Public

   School Adult Education, 1969. 27p. ED 042 084.

   Reported here are the results of a survey regarding
policy statements relevant to professional development
activities and procedures employed to upgrade adult educators. The National Association for Public School
Adult Education (NAPSAE) conducted the survey. Universities sponsoring graduate programs for degrees in continuing education had more explicit objectives outlined
than did professional associations. NAPSAE advocates
professional development of adult educators through degree
granting university programs. Towards this end, the
Committee recommends the establishment of a nationwide
program of fellowships, internships, a public information
system, citizen leadership teams, and others.

436. Robertson, William O., and Dohner, Charles W. Study of
     Continuing Medical Education for the Purpose of
     Establishing a Demonstration Center for Continuing
     Education in the Pacific Northwest. Final Report.
     Seattle: University of Washington School of Medicine,
     1970. 324p. ED 052 323.

    This study describes in detail techniques used to
accomplish the goal of setting up a demonstration center
for continuing medical education. Several objectives
formulated to reach this goal are to: 1) define the education needs of doctors in the Pacific Northwest; 2) evaluate available resources to meet those needs; 3) determine
educational programs for those needs; 4) develop methods
of evaluation; 5) identify participation by doctors;
6) evaluate continuing education programs; and 7) develop
an overall plan for a continuing medical education center.

437. Rogers, Carl R. Freedom to Learn. Columbus, Ohio:
     Charles E. Merrill Publishing Co., 1969. 358p.

    Although primarily known as a psychotherapist, Carl
Rogers is also a teacher. He is interested in the potential within each individual and feels that education is
at a crisis point and in desperate need of change. The
first two sections of the book are practical in offering
approaches in which teachers can attempt experimentation
with their classes whether they be at the elementary
secondary, or university level. The third section outlines the conceptual basis for such experimentation.
Section Four discusses the philosophical underpinnings of
the method. Part Five suggests a program for instituting
self-directed change in an educational system and the
implementation of this program.

438. Rouch, Mark A., ed. <u>Toward a Strategy in Continuing Education: Proceedings of the Consultation on Continuing Education for Ministers of the United Methodist Church, University of Chicago, October 20-23, 1968</u>. New York: United Methodist Church, 1969. 122p. ED 030 036.

As the title indicates representatives of the United Methodist Church make several recommendations for the continuing education of their ministry. The first paper is concerned with general trends in continuing professional education. The second deals with the minister as a professional. A third paper gives the results of a national survey of the profiles of ministers who have participated in continuing education. A fourth paper discusses cybernation and its impact for loss of meaning of the human role. The members set forth objectives for implementing a strategy for continuing education.

439. Schroeder, Wayne L. <u>Concerns about Adult Education</u>, 1968. 14p. ED 023 982.

A national survey (1961-62) reveals that only one adult out of five participates annually in educational activities. The graduate's negative attitude toward education needs to be replaced by an appreciation of life-long learning. Some weaknesses might be overcome through introduction of adult education programs in universities as well as off-campus in-service training and degree programs and establishment of community councils for coordinating the various aspects of adult education. At present, the efforts of adult education agencies are fragmented and no one seems willing to assume a leadership role. Public agencies of adult education should have a system for continuous and reliable data collection, and broader and more balanced programs.

440. Smith, L. L. Mid-Career Education for Urban Administrators

Prepared for the 1969 National Conference of the

American Society for Public Administration, 1968.

ED 029 219.

A mid-career education program for local city administrators is necessary to meet complex and changing
urban needs. Presented is a proposed year-long program
for government officials and key private citizens with
comments on curriculum, instructional methods, participants
and financing.

441. Smith, Robert M.; Aker, George F.; and Kidd, J. R.,

editors. Handbook of Adult Education. New York:

Macmillan Co., 1970. 594p.

This handbook is directed to several audiences--to
any interested person seeking information about adult education, to the part-time worker, to the professional
worker, the scholar, and the graduate student in training. The paucity of data concerning the field of adult
education as a whole and its various components means
there are few reliable statistics. A section is devoted
to professional associations and their impact on adult
education, higher adult education, and professional continuing education.

442. Stout, Ronald M., ed. Local Government In-service Training

An Annotated Bibliography. Albany: State University

of New York, 1968. 88p. ED 028 332.

The bibliography on in-service training is divided
into four major categories: local government training
in general, training generalist officials and administrators, training personnel in functional fields,
and bibliographies.

443. <u>Toward a Learning Society: Alternative Channels to Life</u>,

   <u>Work, and Service</u>. Carnegie Commission on Higher

   Education. Berkeley, California: McGraw-Hill Book

   Co., 1973. 124p. ED 088 373.

   This report is concerned with the place of "non-
   traditional" students within higher education and the
   enhanced role of "further education." The Commission
   favors opening up more options for students outside colleges and universities, more opportunities for returnees
   to higher education and programs for all adults who wish
   to participate in post-secondary education.

444. U.S. National Institute of Mental Health. <u>Annotated</u>

   <u>Bibliography on In-Service Training for Key Pro-</u>

   <u>fessionals in Community Mental Health</u>. Washington,

   D.C.: U.S. Government Printing Office, 1969. 59p.

   ED 037 355.

   Abstracted are 189 documents published between 1960
   and 1967. Documents are listed under the following categories: "Background," "Legislation," "Planning,"
   "Services," "Grants," "Manpower," "Roles of Organizations
   and Key Professional," "Training--In-Service, Postgraduate
   Staff Development," "Training--Residency and Academic
   Credit," and "Brochures and Curriculum Outlines." Also
   included is a subject index to the bibliography.

445.   U.S. National Institute of Mental Health.   Training

       Methodology: Part IV: Audiovisual Theory, Aids and

       Equipment, An Annotated Bibliography.   Washington,

       D.C.:   U.S. Government Printing Office, 1969.   124p.

       ED 023 981.

       This publication is the fourth part of a bibliography
on training methodology within a more expanded series on
mental health in-service and training methodology.   Included are 332 resumes, abstracts, and annotations of
selected documents on audiovisual methods and theory,
facilities, aids, and equipment.   Some of the subjects
covered are: film instruction and equipment, videotape
and sound recordings, television instruction and equipment, graphic aids, multimedia instruction, programmed
instruction, computer assisted instruction, and program
administration and evaluation.

446.   Verner, Coolie.   "Thomas Jefferson."   Convergence.   3

       (no. 4, 1970), 88-90.

       Thomas Jefferson "was a very useful genius."   Through-
out his life, Jefferson believed that the vitality of
democracy rested upon men of reason and good will.   Society
could not long remain ignorant and free.   He saw education
as an integral function of government and fostered free
public education in his native State of Virginia.
Excerpts are presented from the Bill of 1779 which
Jefferson drafted stating his philosophy on public education.

447.   Verner, Coolie, and others.   The Preparation of Adult Edu-

       cators: A Selected Review of the Literature Produced

       in North   America.   Adult Education Association of

       U.S.A., Syracuse University, New York: ERIC Clearing-

       house on Adult Education, 1970. 89p. ED 041 180.

This literature review on the preparation of professional adult educators attempts to cover the leading
areas of discussion and research as well as some of the
more interesting conclusions in the reports. Six major
preoccupations of research are outlined, followed by
two chapters on adult education as a discipline and a profession, patterns of adult educational leadership, levels
and categories of adult educators, and their learning
needs. The document includes a 118 item bibliography.

448. Whipple, James B. Community Service and Continuing

Education: A Literature Review. Occasional Papers,

no. 21. Syracuse University, New York: ERIC

Clearinghouse on Adult Education, 1970. 76p.

This volume analyzes literature in the ERIC
Clearinghouse/AE dealing with Title I of the Higher Education Act of 1966; it includes ninety-two abstracts.

449. Williams, Jack K., Andrews, Grover J. The Continuing

Education Unit and Adult Education. Washington, D.C.:

Adult Education Association of U.S.A., 1973. 17p.

ED 086 868.

The Continuing Education Unit (CEU) is a uniform
nationally accepted unit that provides a mechanism by
which many continuing education activities can be measured
and recorded. A demonstration of the CEU was given at
the National Adult Education Association Conference held
in October, 1973. The National Task Force developed the
CEU in 1968 to determine the feasibility of a uniform unit
of measurement which can be applied to vocational training,
adult liberal education, and professional continuing education as well as other adult/continuing education programs.

Specifically, administrative requirements were laid out for setting up and maintaining quality control over assignment of the CEU. Also covered were the use and criteria of the CEU in the recent Standard Nine provisions of the College Commission of the Southern Association of Colleges and Schools. The National Task Force also presents more detailed outlines on the latest national developments. The Federation of Regional Accrediting Commissions of Higher Education has a workin paper on CEU included in this report. Higher education institutions need to prepare for adult education programs, a predicted major factor in American higher education during the seventies and eighties.

AUTHOR INDEX

(Where citations do not have individual authors, they are
listed under the sponsoring or publishing agency. Numbers
refer to items, not pages.)

A

Abrahamson, Stephen, 333.
Adams, Hobart Warren, 342.
Adams, Kathryn, 226.
Adams, S., 1.
Adult Education Association
of the U.S.A., 343.
Aker, George F., 345, 441.
Alderman, Everett, 374.
Allen, Lawrence A., 2-5,
124.
Alvarez, Robert S., 6, 7.
American Association of
School Librarians, 8, 9.
American Institute of
Certified Public
Accountants, 346.
American Libraries, 164,
225, 258, 265, 281.
American Library
Association, 10-16,
227-232.
Andrews, Grover J., 449.
Asheim, Lester, 18, 19.
Aslib Proceedings, 49.
Association of American
Library Schools,
20-25, 347.
Association of Research
Libraries, 26-28.

B

Barrett, Gerald V., 348.
Barzun, Jacques, 29.
Beacock, E. Stanley, 286.

Belzer, Jack, 30.
Bennett, H. H., 31.
Bewley, Lois M., 287.
Bibliothekar, 306, 320.
Blackstone, Peggy L., 414.
Blake, Fay M., 105.
Boaz, Martha, 7, 32, 33.
Bobinski, George S., 34.
Boelke, Joanne, 35.
Bone, Larry E., 36, 288.
Bookmark, 206.
Booz, Allen and Hamilton,
Inc., 37.
Borg, Walter R., 349.
Bottcher, W., 289.
Botzman, Harvey, 350.
Breivak, Patricia Senn,
38, 39.
Brodman, Estelle, 40, 41.
Brown, Carol A., 81.
Bundy, Mary Lee, 42.
Burgess, Paul, 351.
Burnham, Reba M., 43.

C

Cadence, 394.
California Librarian, 278.
California University, 352.
Carlson, Robert A., 353.
Carnegie Commission on Higher
Education, 354, 443.
Carpenter, C. Ray, 420.
Case, Robert N., 44.
Center for Documentation and
Communication Research, 45.
Charters, Alexander N., 355.

temp card